IMAGES
of America

BAHÁ'Í TEMPLE

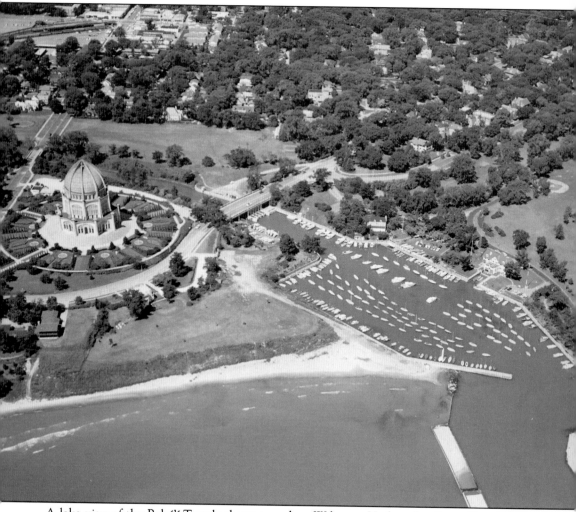

A lake view of the Bahá'í Temple shows a modern Wilmette Harbor, the Coast Guard Rescue Station, and the Sheridan Shore Yacht Club. The empty land directly south of the harbor was made with soil dredged up during construction. The Chicago Transit Authority elevated tracks are west on Linden Avenue, on the top left, which end at the original Linden Avenue station. (Courtesy of the National Spiritual Assembly of the Bahá'ís of the United States.)

ON THE COVER: Pictured is the Bahá'í House of Worship on a summer's day, about 1960 as the Chinese Juniper trees in the gardens are not yet at full height. The aerial photograph shows a busy Sheridan Road, sail boats in Lake Michigan, cranes at the Wilmette Harbor, a full parking lot near the locks of the North Shore Channel, and the greens of the Peter Jans Golf Course. (Courtesy of the National Spiritual Assembly of the Bahá'ís of the United States.)

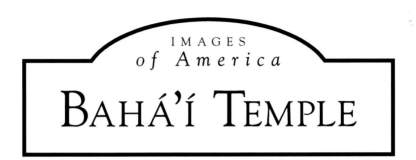

IMAGES

of America

BAHÁ'Í TEMPLE

Candace Moore Hill

ARCADIA
PUBLISHING

Published by Arcadia Publishing
Charleston, South Carolina

Printed in the United States of America

Library of Congress Control Number: 2010923486

For all general information contact Arcadia Publishing at:
Telephone 843-853-2070
Fax 843-853-0044
E-mail sales@arcadiapublishing.com
For customer service and orders:
Toll-Free 1-888-313-2665

Visit us on the Internet at www.arcadiapublishing.com

*For Richard Hill who is my good husband and an editor
for the ages. And for Colin and Laurel who are never
surprised at what happens next in our family.*

CONTENTS

ACKNOWLEDGMENTS

The round foundation building that supports the Bahá'í House of Worship also houses many small offices, some of them hidden away around corridors and behind displays. The people working there have an intimate knowledge of the building they serve and are unfailingly generous with their time and encouragement:

In the Bahá'í Archives, Roger Dahl and Lewis Walker brought file after file of historical photographs to be admired.

In the Bahá'í Media Services studio, Craig Rothman and his staff shared servers full of digital photographs.

With the Heritage Project, Dr. Duane Troxel and Dr. Odmaa Dugersuren were generous with resource material, spiritual and digital.

In the House of Worship Activities Office, Karen Bermann-Mazibuko and her gracious staff cheerfully welcome all visitors, writers, and tourists alike.

Throughout Wilmette, there were many friends eager to render assistance:

At the Bahá'í Publishing Trust and Distribution Service, manager Tim Moore welcomed research and publishing questions.

At the Armbruster Company, Pat and Bob Armbruster flung open the files of the Temple Conservation Library and offered all they had to share, including important technical terms and information.

With Bahá'í Periodicals, editors James Humphrey and Eric van Zanten shared extensive photographic files and their scanner.

At the Wilmette History Museum, curator Patrick Leary showed me original documents from decades past and photocopied anything I wanted.

At the Wilmette Public Library, research librarian Karen Miller found and scanned historical photographs of Fourth and Linden.

My source for exact spelling and usage for Bahá'í terms was *A Concise Encyclopedia of the Bahá'í Faith* by Peter Smith, 2000, from Oneworld Publications, Oxford.

The Man who made Concrete Beautiful by Frederick W. Cron was an invaluable source for the life and artistry of John Joseph Early, 1977, Centennial Publications, Ft. Collins, Colorado.

This book could not have been written without constant reference to the *Dawning Place*, written in 1984 by Bruce W. Whitmore for the Bahá'í Publishing Trust. He spent many years researching the stories that I've condensed to mere captions. To know the whole story about the Bahá'í Temple, find a copy of "Bruce's book."

Unless otherwise noted, all photographs are published by permission of the National Spiritual Assembly of the Bahá'ís of the United States.

INTRODUCTION

The Bahá'í House of Worship in Wilmette, Illinois, has a formal name in Arabic. It is the Mashriqu'l-Adhkár, "the dawning place of the mention of God." The Bahá'í House of Worship is the central edifice of an institution that will eventually include educational, social, and humanitarian agencies. For those living in Chicago-land, it is known as the Bahá'í Temple, the site of a thousand field trips, a short walk through lovely gardens, an uplifting place for silent prayer and meditation, and in 2008 one of the Seven Wonders of Illinois.

It was 1903 when the first glimmers of the idea of a place of worship dawned upon the small group of early believers in Chicago. It began with an inspirational letter from Bahá'í friends in Ashkhabad, which is now called Ashgabat in Turkmenistan. That large and busy Bahá'í community was in the process of building the world's first Bahá'í House of Worship. The Chicagoans knew just a few handfuls of other Bahá'ís scattered across the Eastern United States, mostly in New York and New Jersey. The Midwest hosted small communities in Kenosha, Wisconsin, and Cincinnati, Ohio. There were also a few Bahá'ís on the West Coast, located in California. The idea of their own Temple gave them something to write to each other about, to get excited about, and to allow them to dream big.

In 1907, a petition traveled across America and Canada expressing the desire to build their own Mashriqu'l-Adhkár. More than 1,800 Bahá'ís living in 28 states, the District of Columbia, Canada, and the Hawaiian Islands signed it. When Corinne True, a believer from Chicago, traveled in 1907 to visit the Bahá'ís of Akka in Syrian Palestine, she presented the petition to 'Abdu'l-Bahá, the leader of the Bahá'ís of the world. She was given in return the first instructions for what the building should look like, which included a dome, nine sides, and nine gardens.

Many letters were written across the oceans, and photographs were passed from hand to hand. Funds were donated from all over the world, and land was purchased plot by plot. In 1912, 'Abdu'l-Bahá himself set the cornerstone in an empty field in Wilmette, Illinois, and proclaimed to those present "the Temple is already built." It took more than 30 years before it was done, from the first foundation in 1920 to the last tulip in the gardens in 1954. And here it stands today, the "Great Bell" looking over Lake Michigan, a beacon to airline pilots and boaters, a total surprise to travelers as they drive by on Sheridan Road.

When the completed building was dedicated in 1953, the Bahá'í Faith had spread throughout the western hemisphere. There were elected local Spiritual Assemblies throughout the country and National Spiritual Assemblies in the United States, Canada, Mexico, and many countries of the Caribbean. Future Houses of Worship were being planned for Europe and Africa, which also saw large growth in the number of Bahá'í communities. Today there are about 167,000 Bahá'ís in the United States and more than 5 million across the world. It is often remarked that it was not the fledgling Bahá'í community that built the Temple, but rather their sacrifice to raise the Temple that built the early Bahá'í community.

Residents will drive past for years wondering what goes on inside such a distinctive building. They are often surprised to learn that the Bahá'í House of Worship is open every day of the year, with a staff ready to welcome visitors. Its sole purpose is to provide a place of prayer and meditation for anyone who wishes to do either. The auditorium is open all the way to the top of the dome, with sunlight streaming through hundreds of windows to a shining red terrazzo floor filled with chairs. There is no altar, only a podium used during programs. There is no clergy in the Bahá'í Faith. No sermons or speeches are made during devotional programs in the Bahá'í House of Worship auditorium, only recitations of verses from the Bahá'í writings and scriptures from other faiths, including the Bible, Quran, Upanishads, and others.

Bahá'ís believe in progressive revelation, meaning that all religions have come from one God to educate a single humanity. They recognize the founders of the world's great religions as messengers of God, including Abraham, Moses, Krishna, Buddha, Zoroaster, Jesus Christ, Muhammad, and others lost to history. Bahá'u'lláh (1817–1892) is recognized by Bahá'ís as the latest of these Divine Messengers, the Promised One for this age. This belief is reflected in the designs seen on the Temple's pylons where symbols of many religions are intertwined. The architect of the Temple, Louis Bourgeois, wrote, "In the tracery of the towers are intertwined all the religious symbols of the past, demonstrating to each beholder of any religion: welcome to this Temple exemplifying universal brotherhood."

The Bahá'í House of Worship is described in the Writings of Bahá'u'lláh as following: "O people of the world! Build ye houses of worship throughout the lands in the name of Him Who is the Lord of all religions. Make them as perfect as is possible in the world of being, and adorn them with that which befitteth them, not with images and effigies. Then, with radiance and joy, celebrate therein the praise of your Lord, the Most Compassionate. Verily, by His remembrance the eye is cheered and the heart is filled with light." (*The Kitáb-i-Aqdas*, pages 29, 30.)

There are no special rituals or ceremonies that take place in the Bahá'í House of Worship. Weddings may be held in the gardens or in Foundation Hall under the auditorium level. There are memorial programs but no funerals. The House of Worship Activities Office organizes events, plans devotional services, leads tours, manages volunteer guides, operates a bookstore, and gives special presentations upon request. The building also houses other offices and staff, such as a media center and the Bahá'í Archives.

During the 1933 Chicago's Century of Progress Exposition, the Temple became a tourist destination, worthy of a ride on the El or a car trip up Sheridan Road. It was added to the National Register of Historic Places in 1978 and is mentioned in every Chicago tourism book. The Village of Wilmette is rightly proud of its distinctive character, and images of the Temple have been featured on everything from bus posters to golf course scorecards.

How this building was made is the stuff of novels. There were strong women, surprised men, interracial friendships, last-minute checks in the mail, good fire insurance, Persians in long robes, two world wars, and a Great Depression. The whole story of how it came to be can be told in photographs, of which there are many to choose from. To begin at the beginning, we start at the World's Columbian Exposition in Chicago and the World's Parliament of Religions. It only gets more interesting from there.

One

THE BAHÁ'Í FAITH
COMES TO AMERICA

The very first Bahá'ís were Persian Shí'a Muslims in the 1840s, but within just a few years, Jews, Christians, and Zoroastrians had become Bahá'ís and the faith had spread to Iraq, Egypt, Syria, India, and beyond. One of the first Europeans to chronicle the Bahá'í Faith was British scholar Edward G. Browne, publishing his book *A Year Amongst the Persians* in 1893. His books and articles created interest in the Bahá'í Faith throughout Europe. Browne met Bahá'u'lláh, the prophet-founder of the Bahá'í Faith, in 1890.

Bahá'í belief can be expressed in three main ideas: "That there is only one God, who is the Creator of one human family, and the Source of one religion. These beliefs inform the principles that founders of the great religions were Manifestations of God, all of us are members of one human race, women and men are created equal, education should be universal, science and religion essentially agree, and we are in the process of an ever-advancing civilization that will resolve in world peace."

By the 1890s, Americans began to be exposed to a world that seemed larger and more diverse with every issue of *National Geographic* magazine. There was a curiosity about religions from the East and a fascination with other cultures, languages, and spiritual practices. When an itinerant Syrian arrived in Chicago after the World's Columbia Exposition to teach classes on spiritual healing, there was an interest from open-minded Chicagoans. These were the people who became the first Bahá'ís in America.

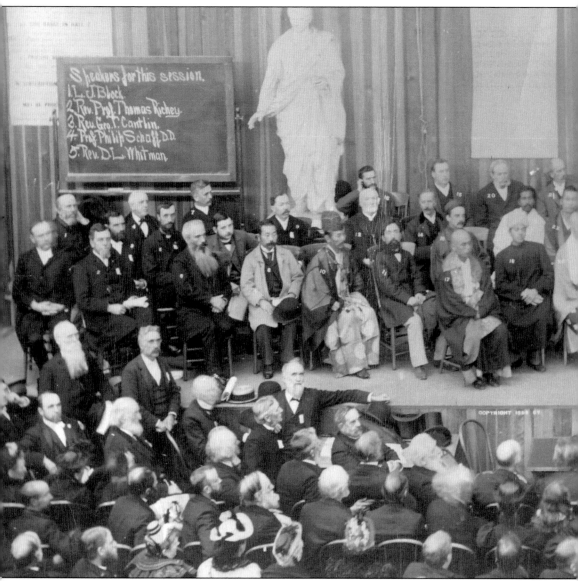

Chicago's World Columbian Exposition in 1893 celebrated the 400th anniversary of the discovery of the New World by Christopher Columbus. The World's Parliament of Religions was one of many conferences planned to coincide with the fair and was the world's first ecumenical meeting. It met for 17 days in the Hall of Columbus at the Art Institute of Chicago. Clergy from many Christian denominations took part, as well as representatives of other faiths, which included the following: Muslim, Hindus, Buddhists, Zoroastrians, Confucians, and Jains. Swami Vivekananda spoke, became a national celebrity, and in 1897 organized the Vedanta Society.

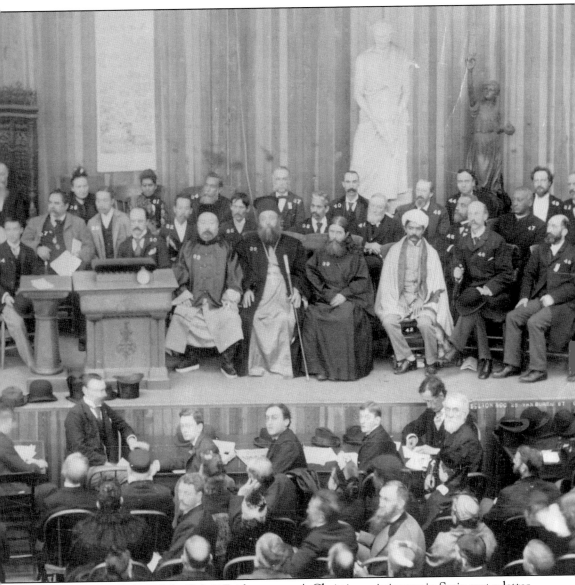

There was no member of the Bahá'í Faith present. A Christian missionary in Syria sent a letter describing Bahá'u'lláh and the Bahá'í Faith that was read at a conference session. The Parliament caused a great interest in comparative religions amongst Chicagoans. When a Syrian Bahá'í named Ibrahim Kheiralla came to Chicago in 1894 hoping to make his fortune, he initiated classes on spiritual healing, which included some Bahá'í prayers and principles. Students in those classes became the early Bahá'ís of Chicago.

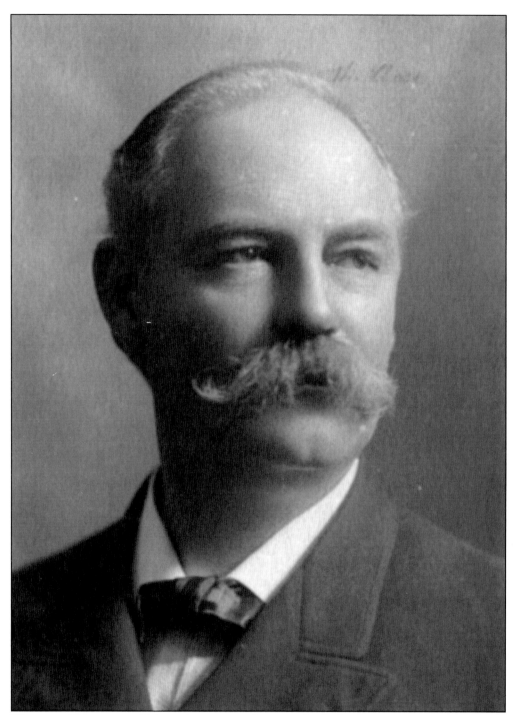

Thornton Chase was a Chicago insurance salesman who had a deep interest in spirituality, reading, and researching multiple world religions before being introduced to Kheiralla at the age of 47. Considered the first American believer, he was the most prominent American Bahá'í from 1894 to his death in California in 1912. In 1900, he initiated the Bahá'í Publishing and Supply Board in order to produce well-written teaching materials.

It is not always possible to identify every person in the photograph collection in the Bahá'í Archives. Thornton Chase, with his striking white mustache, always stands out. Anton Haddad, with his black handlebar mustache, and 'Abdu'l-Karím-i-Tihrání's turban and long beard are also easy to identify. Haddad was a Syrian businessman and the first Bahá'í to visit North America. This photograph would have been taken about 1900.

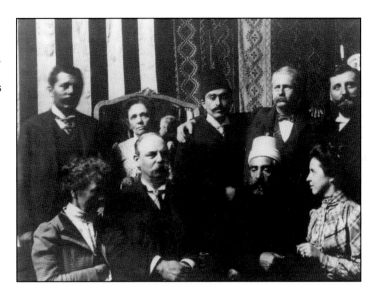

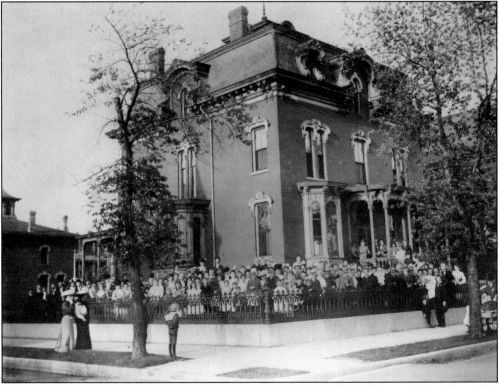

By 1898, the Chicago Bahá'ís had grown to 225 members, most of them having taken Kheiralla's spiritual healing classes in his offices at the Masonic Temple. This group photograph taken in the spring of 1900 shows a man in Persian robes, 'Abdu'l-Karím-i-Tihrání. He was a Bahá'í scholar visiting from Egypt and was sent by 'Abdu'l-Bahá to teach the Americans about Bahá'í history and belief.

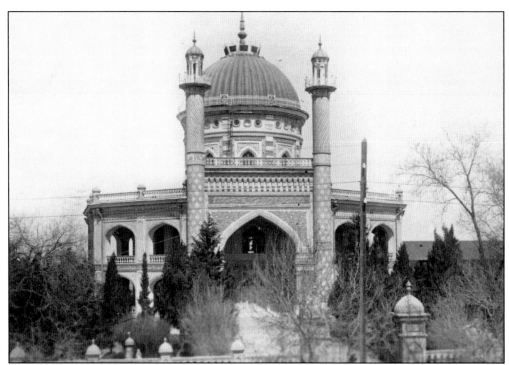

The world's first Mashriqu'l-Adhkár was built in Ashgabat, Turkmenistan, bordering northern Iran. Work began in October 1902 and was mostly completed by 1906, with the ornamentation finished in 1919. Its dependencies included a travelers' hospice; a school for boys, another for girls; two kindergartens; medical dispensary; library; and a public reading room. It served a thriving Bahá'í community of 4,000 people. (Courtesy of the Bahá'í International Community.)

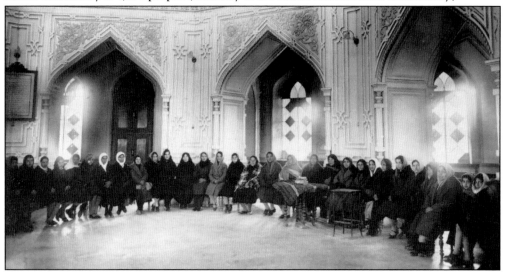

A women's meeting shows the interior design of the Ashgabat Temple. The women and girls would take turns reading or chanting prayers. For modern Iranians in the 1920s, the Bahá'í ideals of education for girls and women's equality were very attractive. While women at this time still wore scarves or veils, several in this picture are in modern clothes with short skirts and stockings. (Courtesy of the Bahá'í International Community.)

14

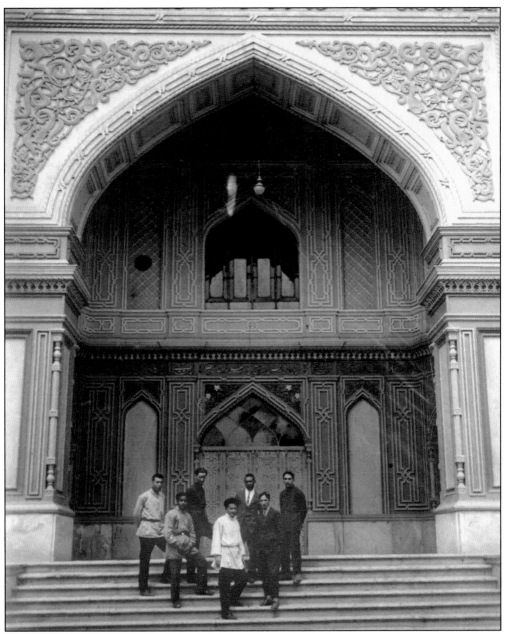

Men posing at the front arch of the Ashgabat House of Worship wear a mix of traditional and modern clothing, showing the diversity of their membership. After the Russian Revolution in 1917, the Bahá'ís were mostly left alone. In 1928, the government confiscated the building, took over the schools, and allowed the community to use the property until 1936. By then, the Bahá'ís were subjected to attacks and arrests, and in 1938, the entire community was forcibly dismantled with most of the members deported, imprisoned, or exiled. The building was closed to the Bahá'ís and turned into a museum. In 1948, an earthquake damaged the complex, and in the 1960s, it was demolished; the site was later turned into a public park. After the fall of the Soviet Union in 1989, Bahá'ís returned to Ashgabat and found believers still resident in the city. (Photograph copyright by the Bahá'í International Community.)

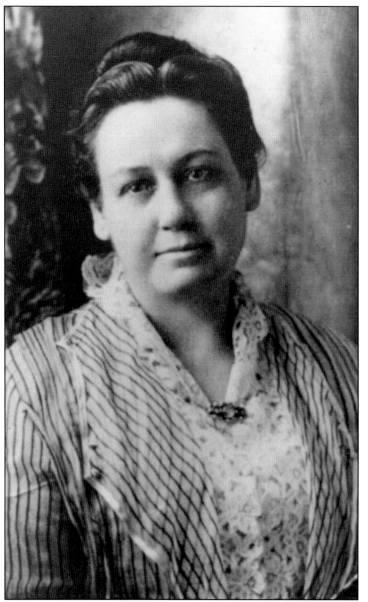

Corinne Knight True became a Bahá'í in 1899. A mother of eight, she began searching for spiritual answers when two of her young children died. She and her husband, Moses True, investigated several new religious movements popular in Chicago. It took but one Bahá'í meeting to win her heart, and she devoted her life to its progress. The project for a Bahá'í Temple captured her imagination, and she knew that it could not be done without coordinated fund-raising. It was she who took a petition in 1907 to 'Abdu'l-Bahá in Haifa asking for permission to purchase the property for a Temple. And it was to her who he gave specific design information about how and where to build, quite confounding Chicago's (men only) Bahá'í House of Spirituality. In 1909, she helped to form Bahá'í Temple Unity, the first Bahá'í organization in America with representatives from different cities and states. She was elected the financial secretary and wrote out every contribution receipt for years afterwards. She lived to see the formal dedication in 1953 and was often called the "Mother of the Temple."

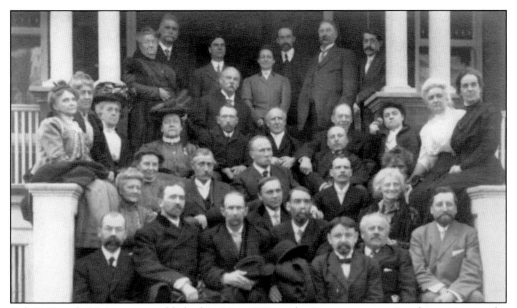

Bahá'í Temple Unity was established in May 1909 as the "permanent national organization for the construction of the Mashriqu'l-Adhkár." Shown here on the porch of Corinne True's home at 5338 Kenmore, delegates from across North America came to Chicago to view prospective sites and discuss their options. At the end of the meeting, they elected a nine-member executive board, including three women.

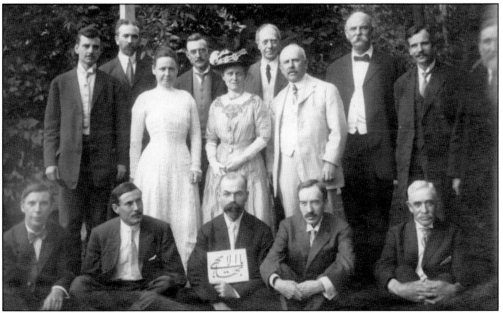

In August 1909, a committee of 15 met to consider design plans for the Temple. The following are, from left to right: (first row, seated) Charles Scheffler, Edward Struven, Arthur Agnew, James W. Woodworth, and George R. Fuller; (second row, standing) Albert Windust, Charles Mason Remey, Corinne True, George Lesch, Ida Brush, Albert Hall, Charles Brush, Thornton Chase, Bernard Jacobsen, and Charles E. Currier. In many photographs of Bahá'ís, one person will hold the "Greatest Name," a calligraphic rendering of a prayer in Arabic.

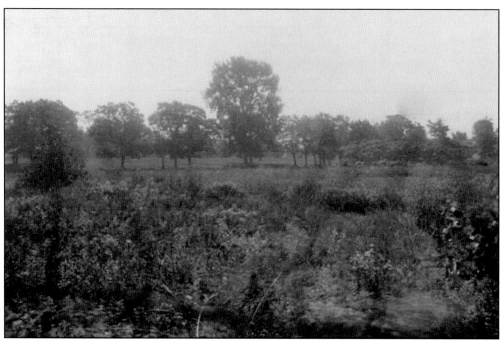

Corinne True and her friend, Cecilia Harrison, rode horsecars up the lakeshore looking at properties. In 1907, they found a large wooded lot overlooking the small natural harbor in Wilmette. This was once part of a reserve set aside for a local Potawatomi woman, Archange, and her husband, Antoine Ouilmette, a French-Canadian fur trader. They had raised a family here and later sold the property to the Village of Wilmette, which was named after these earliest settlers.

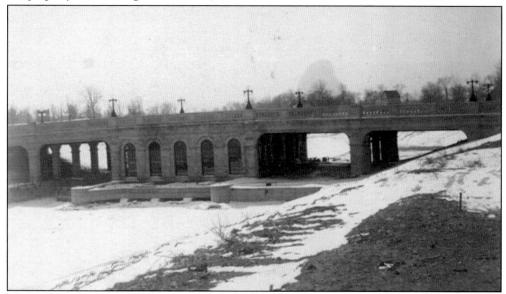

The other large construction project in the area was the North Shore Channel of the Chicago and Sanitary Ship Canal. The channel was dug, and the bridge was built over it for Sheridan Road. Then locks were installed for bringing clean water from the lake to flush Chicago wastewater into the rivers. Land on the other side of the channel was developed into the greens and fairways of a golf course.

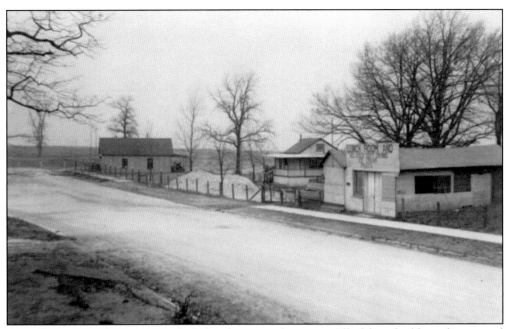

A small commercial area consisted of a lunchroom and a garage. All of these buildings disappeared when noted architect Benjamin Marshall purchased the land to build a fabulous mansion on the harbor. The Bahá'ís also purchased land on both sides of Sheridan Road to protect the lake view.

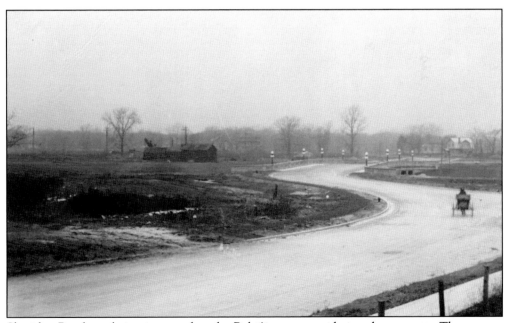

Sheridan Road was being improved as the Bahá'ís were considering the property. There was a concern that the trek from Chicago to Wilmette would be too long, but the remoteness from the city was also a plus, keeping the Temple apart from industrial or commercial areas of the city.

19

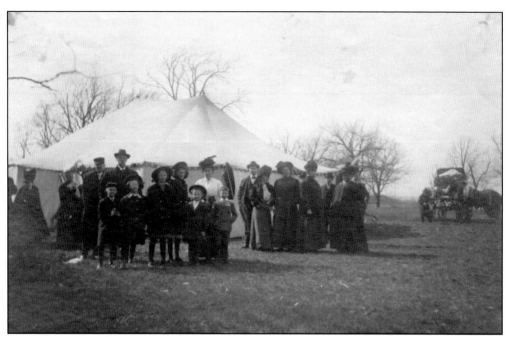

On May 2, 1909, the first lots were purchased and a tent was pitched for a holy day observance. On the back of the photograph is written, "Tent on the Land of the Mashriqu'l-Adhkár," and it was sent from Eva Russell to Gertrude Buikema with the instruction to "please show to the friends in New York and Boston."

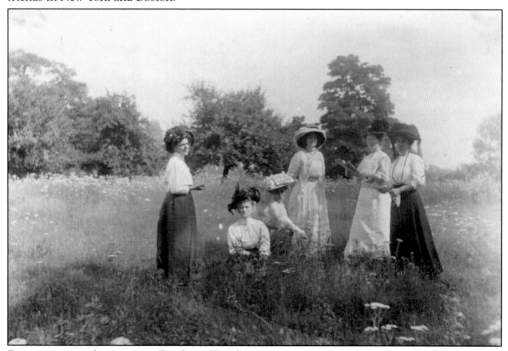

During visits to the property, Eva Russell took many pictures. On July 9, 1909, Elizabeth Diggett, Dr. Susan Moody, Alice Barney, Laura Barney, Jean Masson, and Marie Hopper came to Wilmette to say prayers and pick flowers.

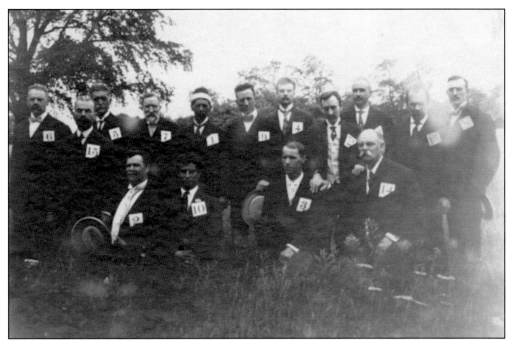

Although they carefully numbered themselves, the list matching these numbers is lost. Chicago's Bahá'í "House of Spirituality" was all men, which included member Thornton Chase, who is kneeling on the right. By 1922, the first women were elected to the Bahá'í National Spiritual Assembly; Corinne True received the highest number of votes overall.

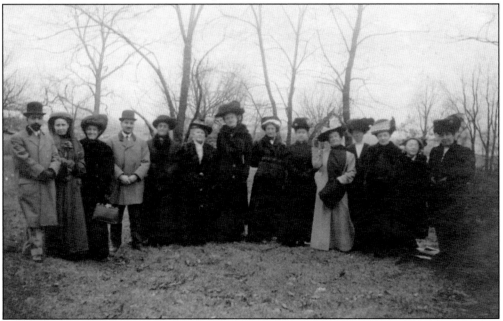

Lua and Edward Getsinger are to the far left in this photograph. Lua Moore attended the spiritual healing classes in 1897 and married Dr. Edward Getsinger shortly thereafter. They were among the first Americans to make a pilgrimage to Haifa in 1898 to meet 'Abdu'l-Bahá. They both returned to the Chicago Bahá'ís with an expanded understanding of Bahá'í history and belief.

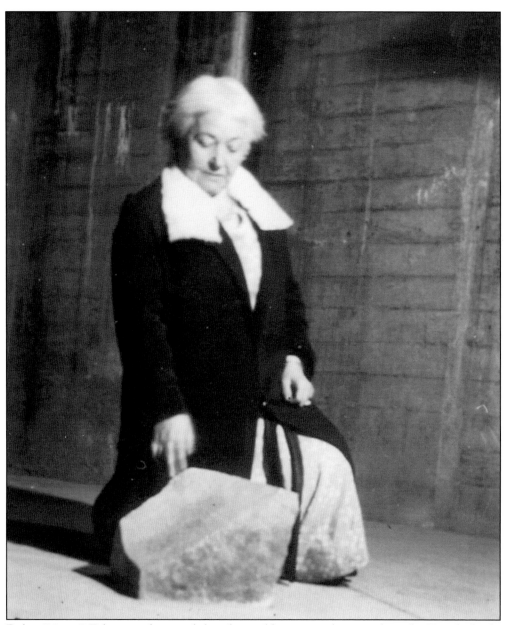

Esther "Nettie" Tobin was distressed that she could not contribute much to the Temple funds. She became a Bahá'í around 1903 and soon was Corinne True's dressmaker. In 1908, a Persian friend wrote, "Now is the time for expending energy and power in the erection of the edifice, be it a mere stone, laid in the name of the Bahá'í Mashriqu'l-Adhkár. For the glory and honor of the first stone is equivalent to all the stones and implements which will later be used there." Inspired, Nettie visited a Chicago construction site and charmed the foreman into giving her a large chunk of limestone from the reject pile. She and a neighbor wrapped the stone in a piece of carpet, then a length of clothesline, and dragged it to her home. More friends helped her drag it to a streetcar, and they ended up at the corner of Ridge and Central in Evanston. It took two days of hauling, which meant leaving the stone overnight in a yard and using a broken-down wooden cart to get it to the Temple property.

Two

'ABDU'L-BAHÁ
COMES TO AMERICA

Upon the death of Bahá'u'lláh in 1892, 'Abdu'l-Bahá Abbas, his eldest son and appointed successor, became the head of the Bahá'í Faith. Born on May 23, 1844, in Iran, he was the exact same age as the Bahá'í Faith, having also begun on the same date. He shared the same fate as his father: exiled to Iraq in 1853, exiled again years later to Constantinople, and again in 1868 to the prison city of Akka in Syrian Palestine along with 67 other friends and family members.

Despite many dangerous years, he was married, and four daughters reached adulthood. The small Bahá'í community in Palestine was able to farm and set up local businesses, although 'Abdu'l-Bahá remained formally a prisoner of the Ottoman Empire. At this time there were Bahá'í communities in Iran, Iraq, India, Egypt, Syria, and throughout the Middle East. By 1906 Europeans and Americans were able to visit Palestine more freely and learn directly from 'Abdu'l-Bahá the essential teachings of the Bahá'í Faith.

As a result of the 1908 Young Turk Revolution, at age 64 'Abdu'l-Bahá was no longer a political prisoner and free to travel. Bahá'ís in Europe, the United States, and Canada begged him to visit, and he spent most of 1911 and 1912 traveling through Egypt, Europe, and then North America. In an era of the public lecture, he sometimes spoke three or four times a day, filling churches and halls across the country.

Howard Colby Ives, a Unitarian minister described 'Abdu'l-Bahá in his 1937 book, *Portals to Freedom* (page 87): "His flowing 'abá, His creamlike fez, His silvery hair and beard, all set Him apart from the Westerners, to whom He spake. But His smile which seemed to embrace us with an overflowing comradeship, His eyes which flashed about the room as if seeking out each individual; His gestures which combined such authority and humility; such wisdom and humor, all conveyed to me, a least, a true human brotherhood."

'Abdu'l-Bahá was a person given to much joy and laughter. "If you are not happy now," he would say "for what time are you waiting?" The American Bahá'ís and their friends alike were astounded by his spirituality, humility, gracious generosity, and the ability to look into the deepest reaches of a seeker's heart. Those who met him considered it the high point of their lives. While the popular press called him a prophet, he referred to himself only as a servant of his father's Faith, hence his name 'Abdu'l-Bahá, which means "the servant of Bahá."

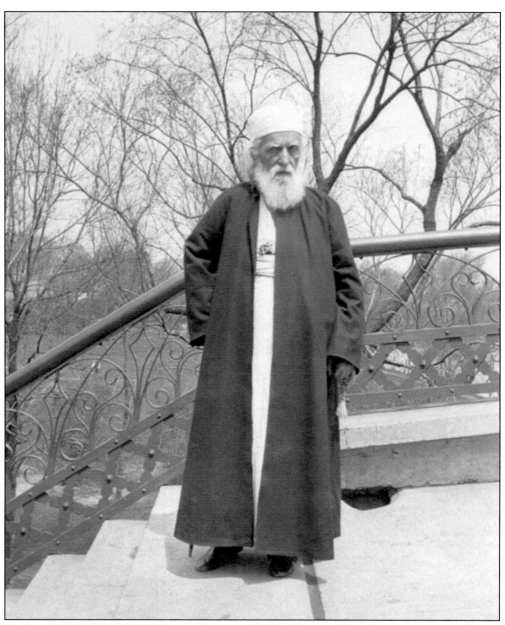

On April 28, 1912, 'Abdu'l-Bahá was 68 years old when he arrived in Chicago. He stayed at the Plaza Hotel where the next morning he met with a large number of Chicago journalists. He visited Jane Addams' Hull House and spoke at the 4th annual meeting of the National Association for the Advancement of Colored People. He spoke again that night to more than a thousand people at a public meeting of the Bahá'í Temple Unity held at the Masonic Temple's Drill Hall. At the end of the meeting, he presented 2,000 francs as his own contribution to the Temple fund. This was a typical day for 'Abdu'l-Bahá. The lobby of the hotel was constantly filled with visitors, and his interpreters reported that there were some who followed him from place to place in their cars in order to hear as many of his talks as possible. On May 4, he spoke to the Theosophical Society at University Hall at Northwestern University in Evanston. Northwestern University Bahá'í students and faculty commemorate this event every year.

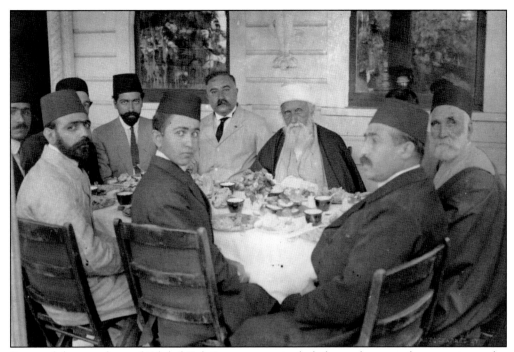

Some of the members of 'Abdu'l-Bahá's entourage included translators and companions who traveled to North America on the *S.S. Cedric* from Egypt. Many of them were already known to the Bahá'ís from their previous visits to the Holy Land.

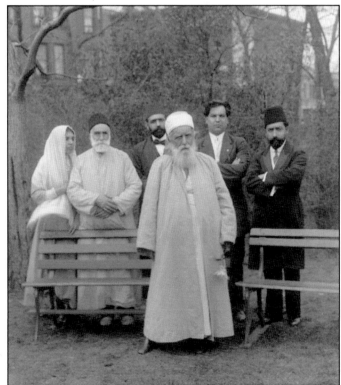

In Lincoln Park, 'Abdu'l-Bahá' posed with his translators and Bahá'ís who were living in the United States as students or visiting scholars. From left to right are Ghodsieh Ashraf, who was the first Persian female student to come to the United States to further her education; Siyyid Assad'llah; Mirza Mahmud, who wrote a diary of these days; Dr. Zia Bagdadi, who lived in Wilmette for many years; and Dr. Amin Farid.

25

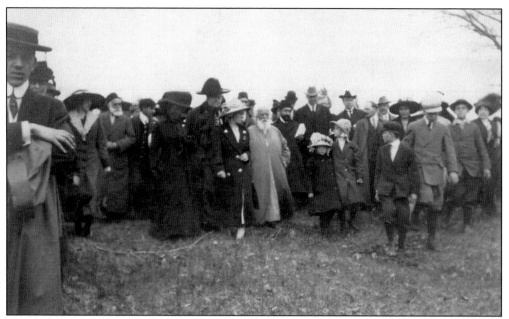

The first day of May was cold and windy. 'Abdu'l-Bahá drove up from Chicago for a dedication program in a tent on the Temple property. When he arrived, Corinne True was waved into the carriage, which then drove to the back of the property. Her son Davis had died of tuberculosis just the day before. A few moments later they walked towards the tent together, and she showed him Nettie Tobin's stone.

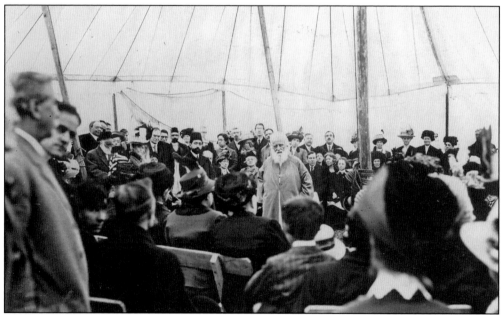

More than 300 people filled the tent, and the prepared program was forgotten. 'Abdu'l-Bahá paced around the center, telling the believers stories about the temple in Ashgabat, about the nine gardens and fountains, and about the future of their Temple that would take them so long to build. "God, willing, when it is completed it will be a paradise." (Promulgation of Universal Peace, page 71.)

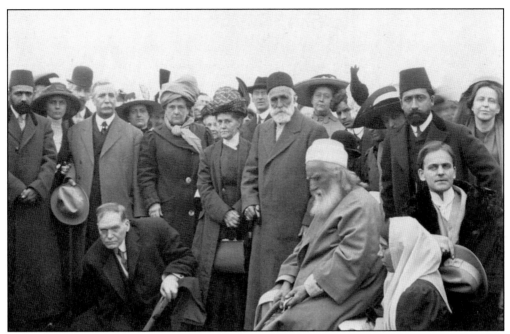

When they left the tent, 'Abdu'l-Bahá was given a small trowel for breaking the earth. Instead, he called for Nettie's stone and sent boys off in search of a shovel and an ax, borrowed from a construction crew. When these were brought back to the assembled group, he swung the axe himself several times to break the earth and then used the shovel to dig a larger hole.

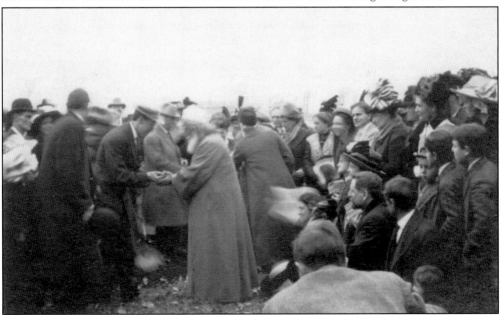

At Corinne True's urging, many people, men and women, took turns with the shovel. Then people were called out of the crowd to represent all the races, cultures, and nationalities present that day. The stone was moved into place on behalf of "all the people of the world." 'Abdu'l-Bahá used the trowel to pat some earth around it and then declared for all to hear "the Temple is already built."

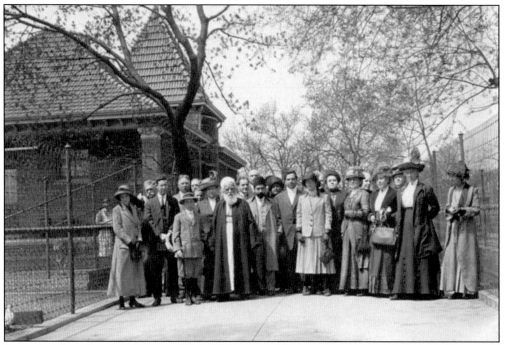

From the Plaza Hotel in Chicago, 'Abdu'l-Bahá could look out onto Lincoln Park, including the city zoo. Several times he took his visitors out to the park for walks, stopping at benches to rest and talk. The Chicago Bahá'ís were very proud to show him the animals at the zoo.

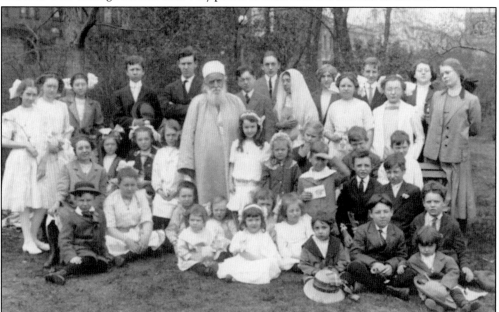

'Abdu'l-Bahá met several times with children, often having sweets for them. He told this group the following: "May you develop so that each one of you shall become imbued with all the virtues of the human world. May you advance in all material and spiritual degrees. May you become learned in sciences, acquire the arts and crafts, prove to be useful members of human society and assist the progress of human civilization." (Promulgation of Universal Peace, page 91.)

Three

CHOOSING A DESIGN

In 1909, the governing board, named Bahá'í Temple Unity, put out a call to architects for design submissions and began to (slowly) raise funds. High hopes led to dismay as World War I and severe recession slowed progress to a crawl. Several architects had hopes of winning the commission, but only one devoted years of his life in the quest for a building that represented his newfound spiritual ideals.

An architect's review of the Temple design would point out that its symmetry was surely influenced by the École Des Beaux Arts. The dome is early Renaissance, with an arabesque tracery common in Islamic architecture. The ribs could be called Gothic, the clerestory suggestive of Romanesque, and the arches over the windows look like 8th-century Moorish Spain. The pylons are reminiscent of the minarets of great Muslim mosques.

The symbols on the pylons represent the great religions and spiritual beliefs from around the world: circles, crescents, triangles, pyramids, the Greek and Roman crosses, the hooked cross, five-, six-, seven-, eight-, and nine-pointed stars, and the sun and moon and their movement in the heavens. It took architect Louis Bourgeois nine years to imagine it, through dreams and visions and a determination to make a brand-new thing that represented all the best of what had come before.

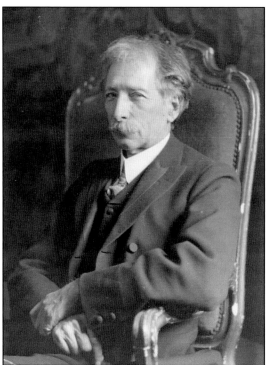

Louis Bourgeois (1856–1930) was a well-traveled French-Canadian architect. He was educated in France and traveled throughout Europe, the Middle East, and to Chicago in 1886 where he worked for firms like Burnham and Root and Holabird and Roche. In the 1890s, he moved to San Francisco to design for the San Francisco World's Fair. By 1906, he was living in New York, where he became a Bahá'í.

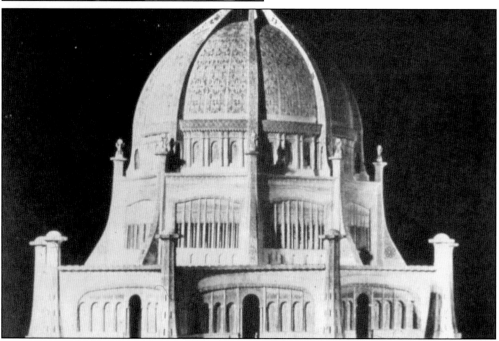

Although he had no training in plasterwork, Bourgeois built this model in 1919. Completely broke, he stripped the garden in front of his house and sold roses on the streets of New York, making just enough cash to buy a barrel of plaster. A friend helped him make the molds and taught him how to cast the dozens of individual pieces. The finished model shows a much larger building than what was eventually constructed.

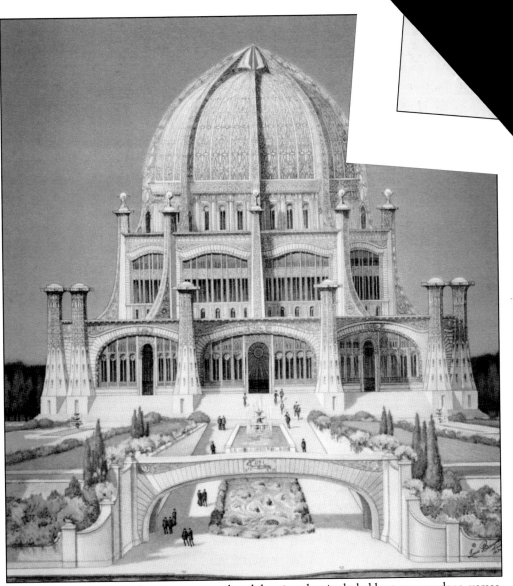

Bourgeois expanded his ideas in a water-colored drawing that included lanterns, gardens, verses, fountains, and a waterway under Sheridan Road to Lake Michigan. Upon winning the contract in 1920, it was reproduced many times, distributed throughout the Bahá'í world, and small versions were presented to workmen on the site. Although many changes and adjustments were made throughout construction, it was this image that cemented the idea of the Bahá'í Temple in the minds of those who raised the funds over the decades it took to build it. The Bahá'í treasury does not accept contributions from non-members. Contributions for the Temple came from every Bahá'í community in the world.

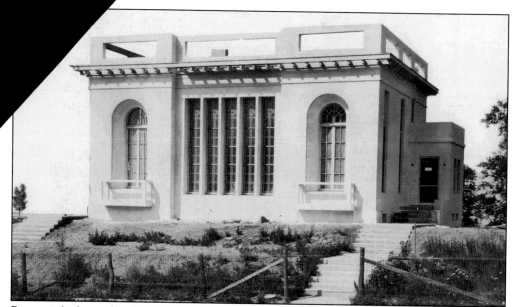

Bourgeois had rented studio space in Chicago, but he soon wanted to be closer to the Temple property. On the land across Sheridan Road, which was purchased to prevent commercial buildings from blocking lake views, he used scrap lumber left over from construction of the foundation to create a new living space for himself. Suspected by some to be an elaborate mansion or Italian villa, the interior featured an open studio with large windows fit for someone working on a detailed project.

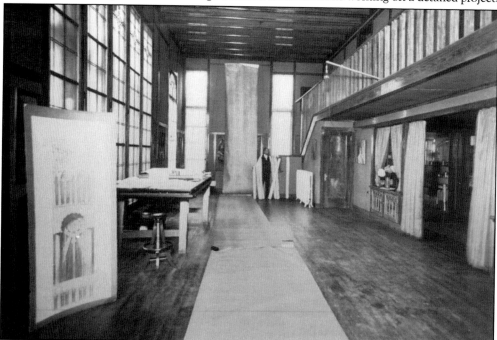

This room was designed to lay out long sheets of paper for drawing the decorative motifs of the Temple. Bourgeois was a master draftsman, drawing incredibly detailed fruits, leaves, arcs, and interlacing lines. Inspired by the paths of the stars as they traveled across the night sky, he wanted the Temple to shine out, a beacon of peace to the world, a great "bell" calling all to prayer.

Four

THE TEMPLE RISES

In 1920, when funds were available, the call for architect submissions was renewed, and several designs and four models were shown at that year's Bahá'í Temple Unity Convention. The end of a long and complex process confirmed the unanimous choice of the Temple of Light by Louis Bourgeois. 'Abdu'l-Bahá suggested that "a smaller one would be better," and so Bourgeois later reduced the size by one-half.

Maj. Henry J. Burt, chief structural engineer of the firm Holabird and Roche, was hired to ensure that all the construction plans were accurate and correct. Before anything could begin, a permit had to be obtained from the Village of Wilmette, which insisted upon detailed and exact plans for what everyone understood was a unique project. There was an objection in the press by some local clergymen, but the Village Board of Trustees was open-minded and looked at the Bourgeois design on its own merits. A permit was issued in March 1921, and the Avery Brundage Company was hired to dig wells 120 feet down to the bedrock and then build the 6-foot-wide concrete foundation caissons.

Once the foundations were done, a building was constructed over them, to protect the foundation and to give the Bahá'ís a place to meet. Foundation Hall, the home of many programs, lectures, and National Conventions, was first used as a meeting place on July 9, 1922. Hopes were that it would not take long to begin work on the steel superstructure. In order to take the next step, it was determined that $400,000 would have to be raised. It took 10 long years to gather those funds.

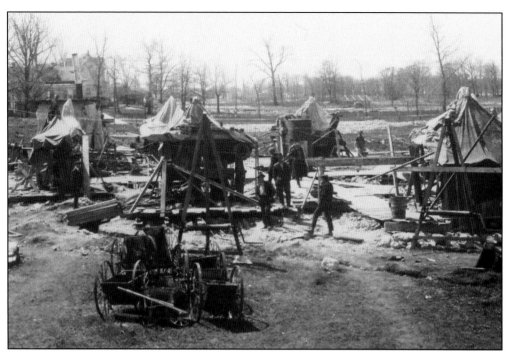

Nine concrete caissons were poured, nearly 12 stories below ground to the bedrock. This large building was constructed to be the basement of the future Temple. The street-level door here looks like an underground entrance in later pictures. The skylights were later replaced with one single skylight in the center. The slope of the roof is where the monumental stairs are today.

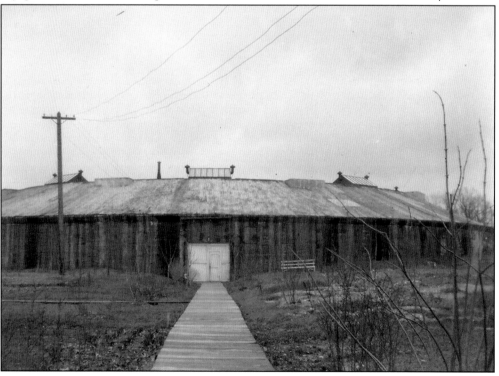

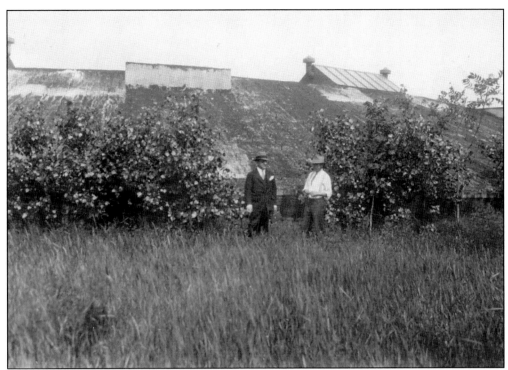

When construction was delayed, the neighbors began to complain about the bleakness of the foundation building. A landscaping program planted hundred of trees and vines, using volunteer weekend labor. Inside the building did not look much better, and soon funds were allocated to make the large meeting room look more finished. The Bahá'ís of Chicago donated the materials for the floor and the first piece of furniture, a table still in use today.

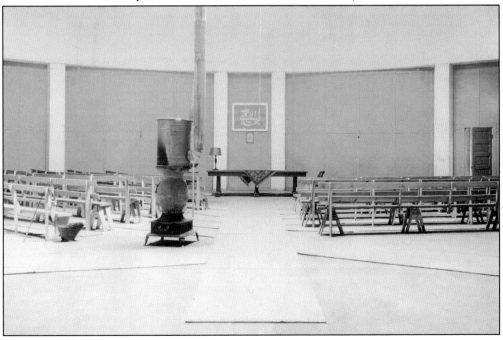

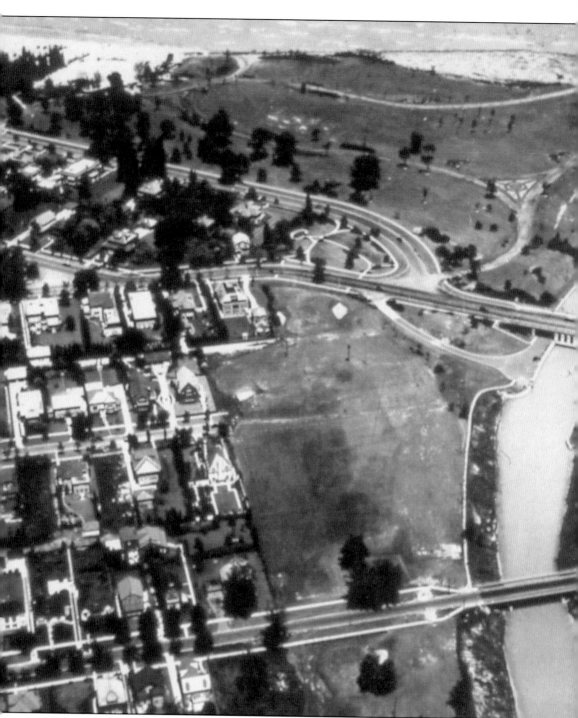

The aerial photograph shows the forlorn-looking foundation building (about 1929) and a rapidly changing lakefront neighborhood. The locks remain under the bridge on Sheridan Road with the hope that boats could use them, but when that became impractical they were later removed. Gilson Park is under development, having received extra land from the channel dredging. The Coast Guard rescue station is not yet built (1931), and the fabulous Marshall mansion on the

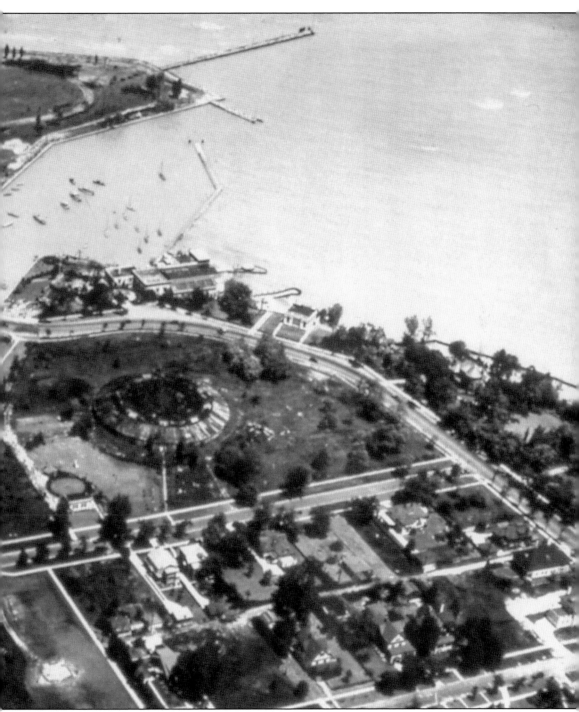

harbor is not yet destroyed by fire and high taxes (1950). When it was demolished, the Bahá'ís purchased the land. The golf course greens look inviting. Some homes on Linden Avenue have yet to be built, but the Bourgeois Studio and the caretaker's home look pretty in white compared to the unattractive foundation building.

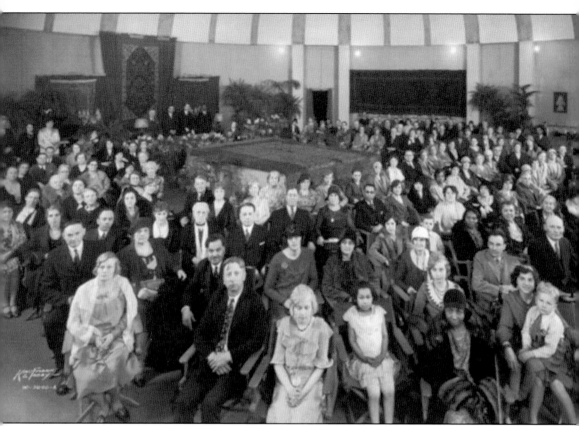

Upon the death of 'Abdu'l-Bahá in 1921, his will and testament appointed his grandson Shoghi Effendi as the Guardian, the new head of the Bahá'í Faith. Corinne True had first met him as a boy of 10 and watched as he grew, attended university in Oxford, England, and became his grandfather's able secretary and translator. Shoghi Effendi followed the building of the Temple with great interest and often made his own monthly pledges as a way to inspire the Americans to meet their fund goals. In 1929, a surprising letter arrived. Looking for ways to encourage and inspire them, he had the Bahá'ís' most precious Persian silk carpet in the Holy Land rolled up and shipped to Chicago. It was his hope that this unique and beautiful object could be sold for as much as $20,000. The stock market crash swept away any interest in valuable Mashhad carpets, but the Bahá'ís responded magnificently, finding it within themselves to make the necessary contributions. The 1930 convention was a victory celebration with the carpet displayed for all to admire.

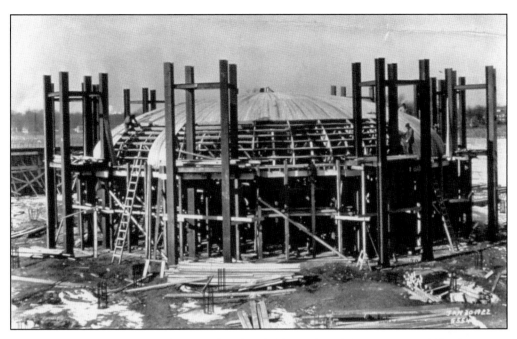

By October 1930, the steel had been ordered and delivered, and the George R. Fuller Company began construction. A crane was constructed on top of the foundation building and an elevator to the side to bring up materials as the structure grew. The Fuller Company, in Chicago since 1883, was one of the first large general contracting firms in the country and was trusted with many stages of the construction of the Baháʼí Temple.

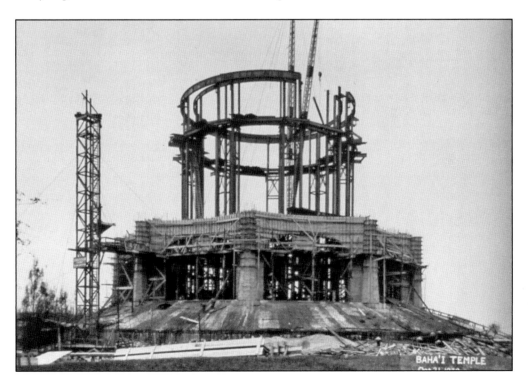

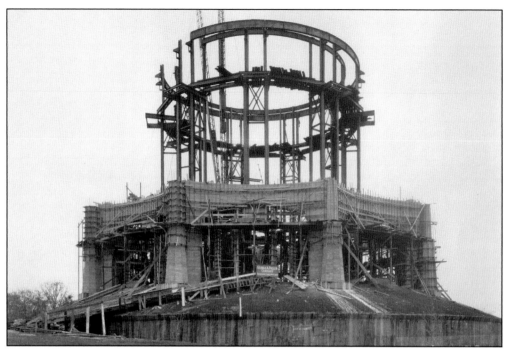

With flowing curves in every direction, a nine-sided structure was not a familiar task for the many competent men figuring out just how to fit together this interesting building. Eventually, a template had to be built on-site; forms for the structural concrete were constructed around it and then transferred to the building one at a time. Despite their best efforts, all nine sides are not quite identical.

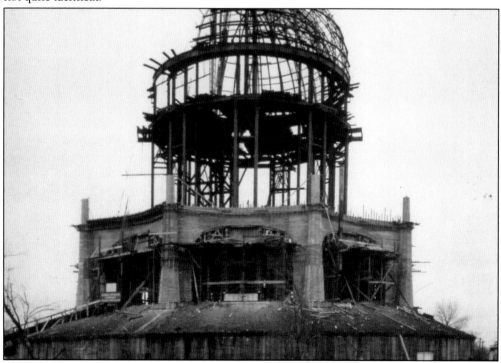

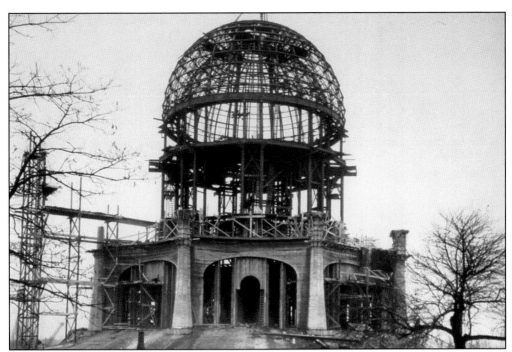

Just when all was going perfectly, a windstorm blew over a heater late at night and lit a fire that required engine companies from Wilmette and Evanston to extinguish it. It was horrible to see but didn't damage much more than the wooden forms. The steel and concrete were not harmed, and the payment from the insurance was more than enough to cover the damage.

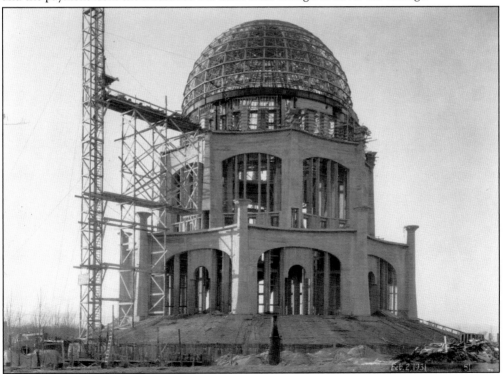

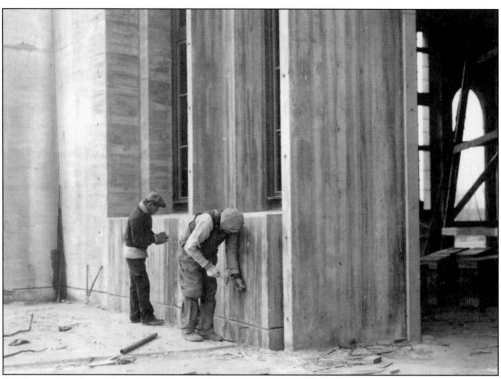

Workmen finishing the concrete work show the scale of each of the nine sides of the building.

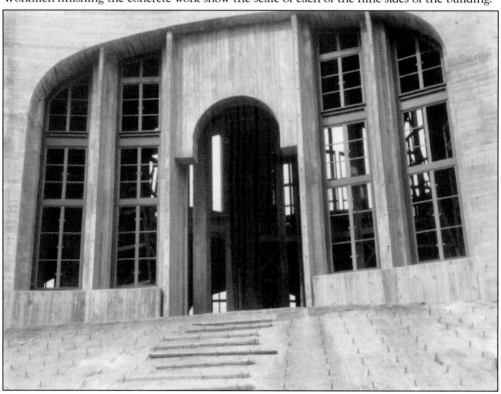

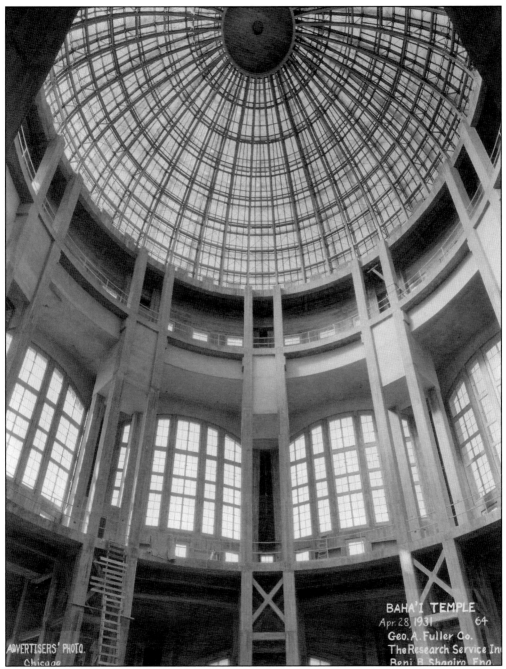

BAHA'I TEMPLE
Apr. 28, 1931   64
Geo. A. Fuller Co.
The Research Service In
Beni B. Shapiro Eng

The interior of the enclosed Temple shows the skylight that will later be covered inside and out with decorative concrete panels. The dome rises 138 feet from the floor of the auditorium. The entire building required 19,500 square feet of glass. On May 1, 1931, the first gathering inside the auditorium was held to dedicate the structure, exactly 19 years to the day from when 'Abdu'l-Bahá laid the cornerstone.

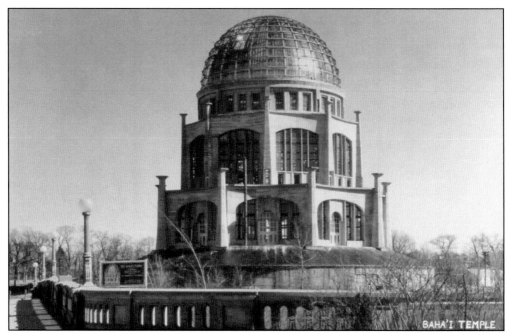

Shown is the completed gray glass "bubble" of the Temple dome, as it would have been seen driving south on Sheridan Road. It is fully enclosed, with wooden doors that would not be replaced for another 20 years. From the street level, it is nearly two stories to the auditorium entrance. At this point in its construction, no one knew exactly how the exterior ornamentation would be made or what it would be made of.

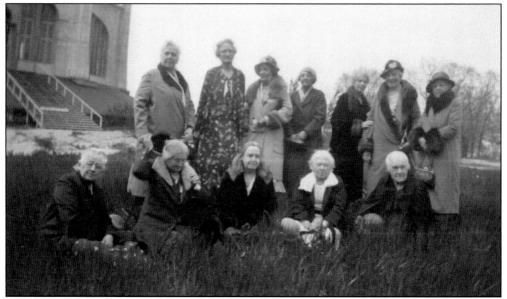

Written on the reverse of this photograph is the following: "These 12 were the oldest pioneers of the Cause to be found in Chicago in May 1932 who came in from 1896 to 1900." Shown here are (first row, seated) Mary Lesch, Rose Robinson, Corinne True, Nettie Tobin, and Sophie Loeding; (second row, standing) Emma Lundberg, Gertrude Buikema, Louise Waite, Fannie Lesch, Lillian James, Elizabeth Greenleaf, and Marie Ioas.

Five

A TEMPLE OF LIGHT

Louis Bourgeois's vision of the Temple of Light was a pure white dome, etched with the reflected paths of planets and stars. It would have huge lamps upon the nine pylons and a giant searchlight at the top of the dome with its beam broken into nine points shining into the darkness. He drew intricate patterns on rolls of paper more than 70 feet long and envisioned a watercourse directly to Lake Michigan so that visitors could arrive in their boats. He died in 1930 at age 74, leaving the Bahá'ís with a dazzling vision, and a few beautifully detailed drawings, but no other architectural plans.

Bourgeois did have an idea how to fashion the decorative elements in this unusual building. In 1920, he visited John J. Earley of the Earley Studio in Washington, D.C., a master craftsman and designer who had invented new processes for the uses of ornamental concrete. They had a meeting of minds as to how dazzling white concrete could be poured into molds and pieced together to make a dome. Earley later said that Bourgeois was "the most unusual personality I have met in the profession." During a visit to his Chicago loft on La Salle Street, Bourgeois tied a pencil "to the end of a long stick, which he drew in great sweeps, in a manner never to be forgotten, the interlacing ornament of the dome. One line through another, under and over, onward and upward until the motif was completed," as stated on page 166 in the book *Dawning Place*.

Consulting with Bourgeois, the Earley Studio prepared a sample mold; worked up a concrete with a mixture of quartz, sand, and Portland cement; and sent a finished panel to Wilmette where it was placed outside to watch how it would weather. It would be 10 years before the studio would receive a contract for the entire dome, but it was no matter. John Earley knew from the beginning that the Bahá'í Temple project was to be his life's greatest work: "A Temple of light with a great pierced dome through which by day the sunlight would stream to enlighten all within and through which by night the Temple light shown out into a darkened world."

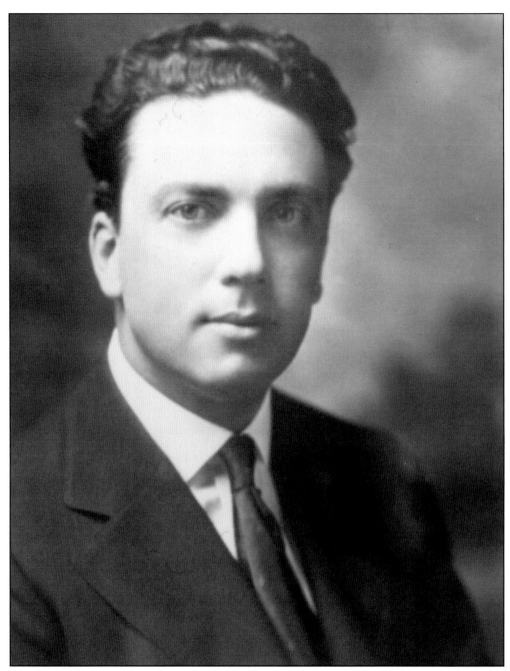

John Joseph Earley was born into a family of sculptors and stone carvers. He inherited the Earley Studio in 1906 and moved from stone to stucco work. He had a long list of credentials, which included working on the interior of the White House. In 1914, he designed research projects for the U.S. Bureau of Standards perfecting building standards for stucco and architectural concrete. His other projects included the Fountain of Time in Chicago in 1922 and the Greek Parthenon in Nashville, Tennessee, in 1925. In 1934, he invented the Polychrome House in Silver Springs, Maryland, the first prefabricated concrete structure, influencing building construction to this day.

John Earley's lifelong business partner was Basil Gordon Taylor, the engineer who would translate the artistic designs into practical construction. It was Taylor who built the full-sized wooden replica of the steel structure of the dome at the studio yard in Rosslyn, Virginia. Only a one-ninth section was required to ensure that every piece would fit perfectly on the dome.

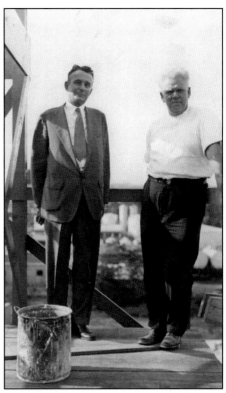

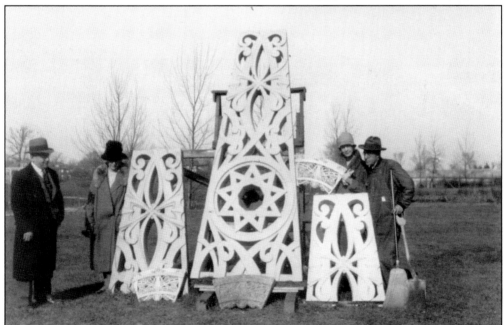

A materials committee had been appointed by Bahá'í Temple Unity to investigate a variety of materials. Terra-cotta, tile, sandstone, aluminum, bronze, and marble had all been evaluated in the 1920s, but none were as malleable as the concrete, and others could not even be priced. These experimental panels were set out on the property to weather in the harsh Chicago climate.

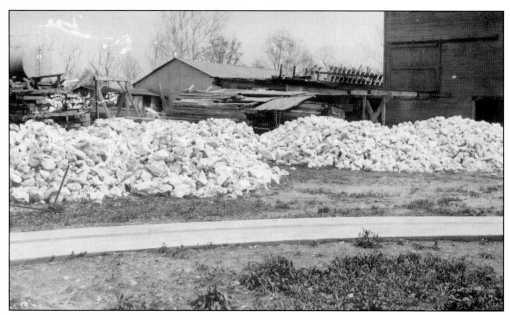

Two kinds of quartz were chosen to create the desired effect. They were crystalline quartz from Spartanburg, South Carolina, and opalescent quartz from Monita, Virginia. The quartz was crushed, screened to a specific size, and mixed with sand and cement to create a bright white architectural concrete.

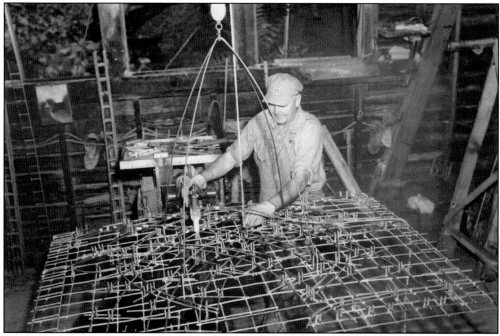

It took 743 tons of quartz to make the panels for the ornamental exterior of the dome. Each panel began with a stainless steel reinforced base, individually composed for each decorative design. Crushing such a large amount of stone required a new workshop, moving from Washington, D.C., to Virginia. Earley and Taylor built a modern and efficient system for producing aggregates to exacting specifications.

Earley Studio's craftsmen laid their carving tools around this large slab of modeling clay, sculpted in reverse, which was the first step in creating the molds. The studio sculptor Leander Weipert was the artisan who translated Louis Bourgeois's designs into the clay. He was so taken by their intricacy that he insisted on carving nearly every mold himself.

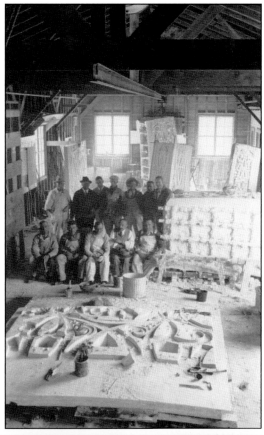

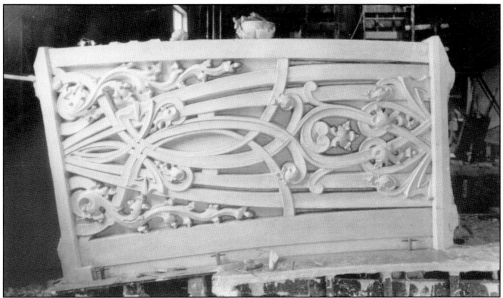

To sharpen the detail and make the lines of the designs as true as possible, Weipert and his assistant carved the first plaster molds. It took 24 different molds to create a total of 388 panels that make up the Temple's ribs and dome.

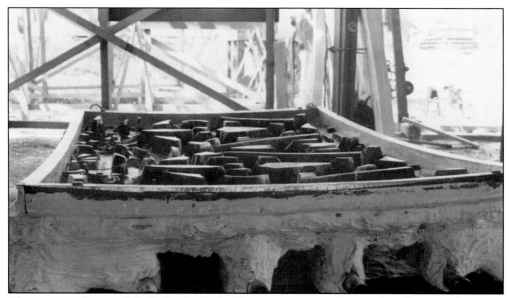

The master craftsmen of the Earley Studio had long experience working with and carving decorative plaster. Clay models were used to make plaster molds. These were then used to make plaster casts that were fitted to the sample section of the dome to ensure a perfect fit. The final molds were lined with a thin zinc coating and then shellacked to withstand repeated usage.

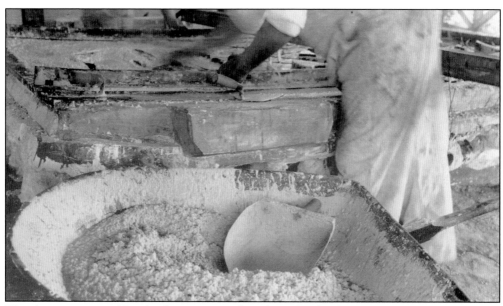

The slurry mixture of Portland cement, sand, and two kinds of quartz was laid into the mold and smoothed. Each mold was hit several times on the sides with wooden clubs to make sure that every little crevice was filled. The molds were then vibrated, again and again, to shake the water out of the mix.

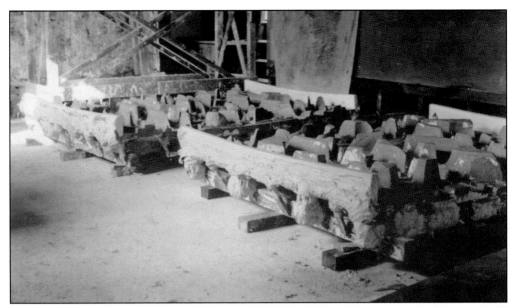

John Earley found that the faster the water was drained from the concrete, the better it held together. He invented a process using pads of paper and cloth that were laid on top of the mix to wick out the moisture.

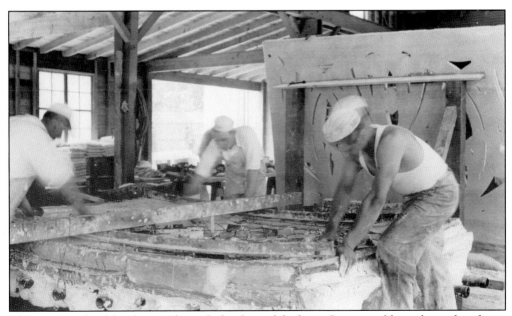

The concrete dried for about 20 hours before being lifted out. Once a mold was deemed perfect it could be used 9, 18, or even 27 times, with every panel a duplicate of the others. This photograph shows the smooth back of one large panel.

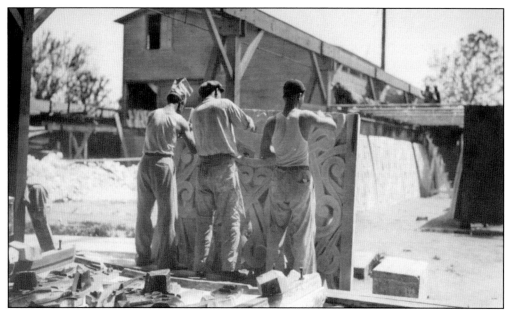

When the "green" panel was lifted from the mold, men were ready with wire brushes and a slightly acidic water mixture to lightly scrub the top layer of mortar from the surface to expose the sparkling quartz.

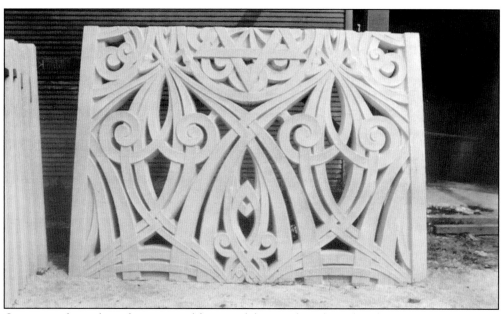

Once a panel was cleaned, it was cured for several days in a huge humidity chamber and then placed for air-drying in the studio's yard. John Earley developed this process, and his workmen were very experienced at it. None of his previous projects had been as detailed and complex, a challenge that kept John Earley and Basil Taylor constantly inventing new methods and designs.

To ensure absolute accuracy, a one-ninth wooden template of the dome was built in the studio yard. Earley knew at once that making large whole sections for the dome would be overly complicated and that larger sections could not contract and expand in response to the wide variations of Chicago's winters and summers.

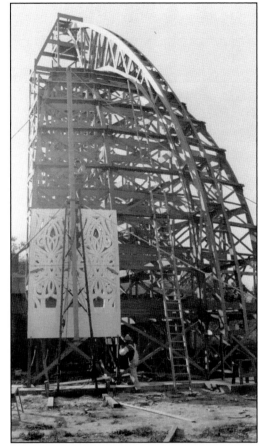

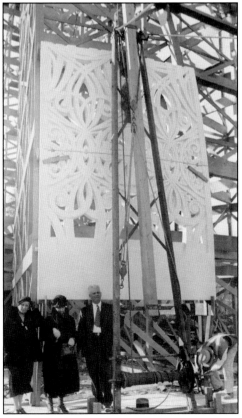

Smaller panels were designed with a half-inch space between them to allow for movement. Each section of the dome and ribs required dozens of individual pieces, each of which was then replicated at least nine times.

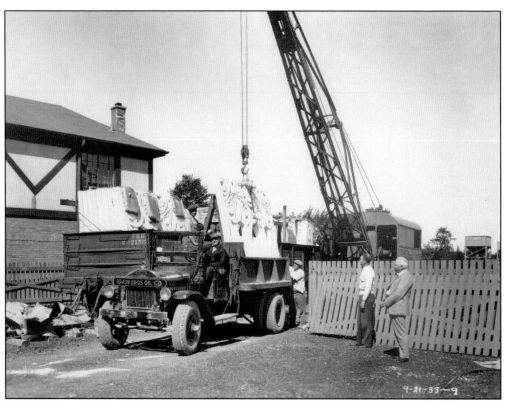

Transporting the dome from Virginia to Illinois required intricate planning. On August 28, 1933, the first trucks were carefully loaded for the drive to the rail yard. Winches and a pulley lifted each piece to be securely stowed on multiple open cars. The reverse took place at a railway siding in Wilmette, and then each piece was unloaded at the Temple grounds.

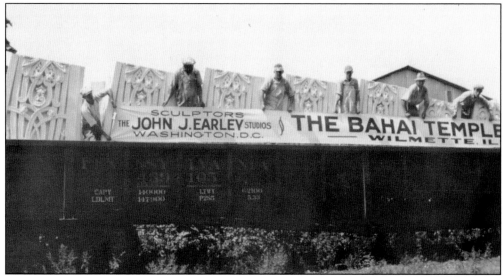

The Earley Studio was very proud and invested in signs to advertise its work. A sign above the workshop in Virginia said, "The Bahá'í Temple Dome, Wilmette, Illinois, The Most Elaborate Concrete Structure in the World."

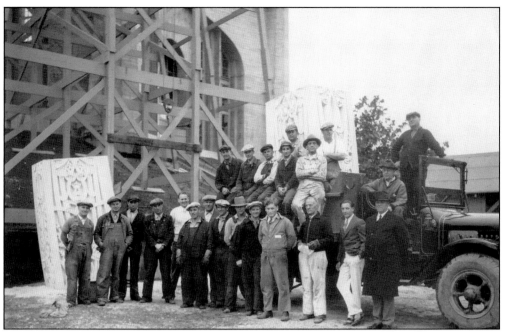

The first trucks arrived, and the Earley Studio's work crew became expert at installing the panels using ingenious systems of cranes, pulleys, and scaffolding. No one remembers whom the sharp young man in coat and tie amidst the experienced craftsmen is, but perhaps he is a college-aged son or a visiting architecture student.

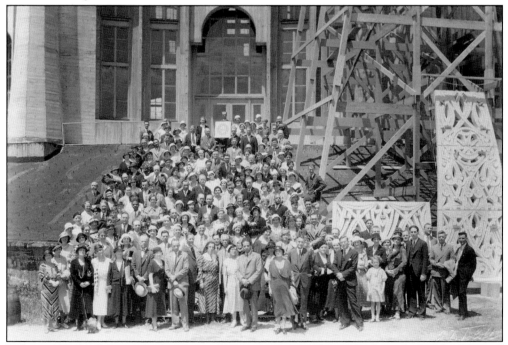

In June 1933, the delegates at the National Convention posed with the first panels to be delivered to Wilmette. In September, the first major shipment arrived. By the end of the month, 260 of the 388 panels had been manufactured, and 76 of these were on the dome.

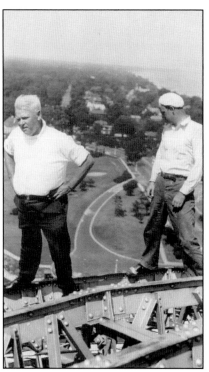

Basil Taylor had surveyed and measured every steel beam. He supervised the setting of each panel and apparently had no fear of heights. Behind him is a stunning view of Lake Michigan, Sheridan Road, and the golf course. The original contract called for the completion of just the dome, but it became clear during construction that the ribs should be built as one piece from their apex down to the roof of the clerestory.

The dome progressed in stages. As more panels were manufactured, they were delivered and installed, all fitting together smoothly.

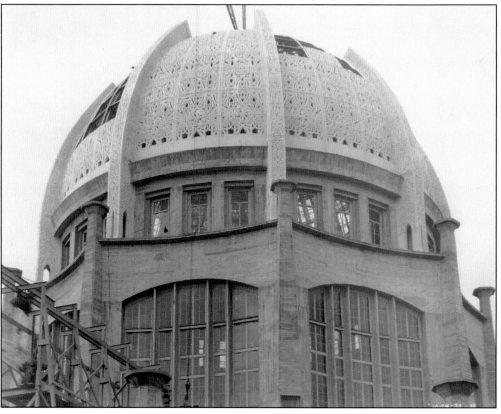

A crane was built on the steel superstructure to bring up each panel. A very close look reveals two workmen riding up with the panel and another to meet them and move it gently into place. Despite severe fund-raising challenges during the Great Depression, the final panel was put in place on March 4, 1934. For the first time, passersby could catch a glimpse of what the finished shape of the building would look like, which was much different than the gray bubble of the last few years.

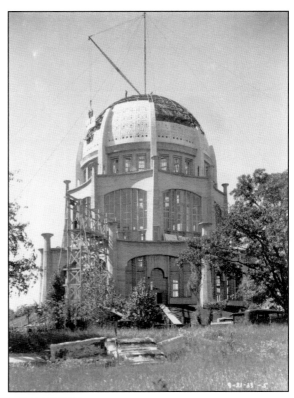

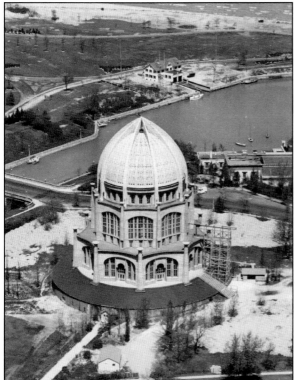

The dome was completed during Chicago's Century of Progress Exposition, and fairgoers often traveled up the lakefront to sightsee. Dr. Rexford Newcomb, dean of the College of Fine and Applied Arts at the University of Illinois, said that it was "not matched by any domical structure since the construction of Michelangelo's dome on the Basilica of Saint Peter in Rome."

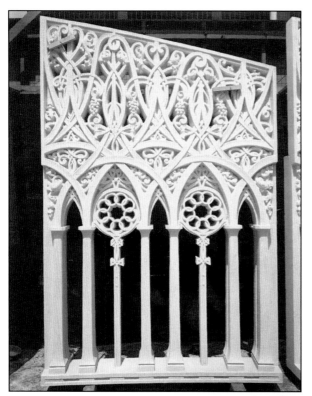

The completion of the dome, the most complex part of the building, encouraged the Bahá'ís' to fund the next level of the project, the clerestory. By May 22, 1934, the first railroad car with 97 panels was on its way from Virginia with installation beginning in June.

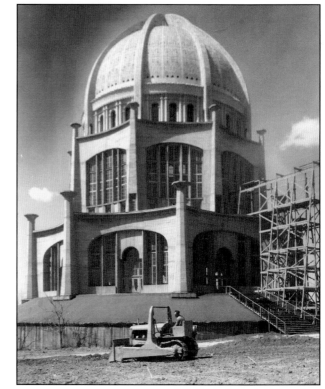

Despite severe winter weather that slowed progress, the clerestory level was finished by July 1935. This was the last time the pure white dome could be seen before dust storms impregnated it with dirt.

It took two more years to raise the money required to begin the next level, the gallery. On this level, some of the ornamentation was cast directly onto the building, and by April 1938, steel, molds, and 54,000 pounds of sand and crushed quartz were delivered to the property. This Earley Studio group photograph includes the milkman on the far right.

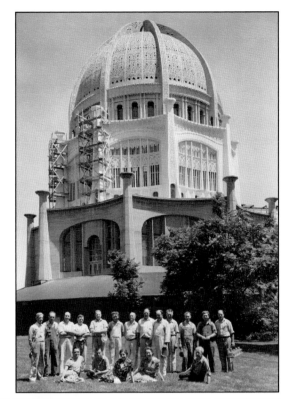

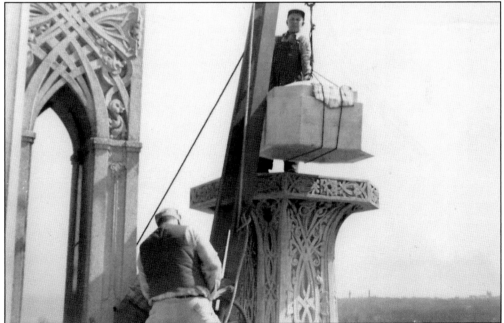

One of the three workmen setting the cap into the pylon is turning a winch by hand. They have a view of the Gross Pointe Lighthouse in Evanston, seen far in the distance along with a smokestack. Louis Bourgeois's vines, leaves, and little nine-pointed stars seem placed there just for them to admire.

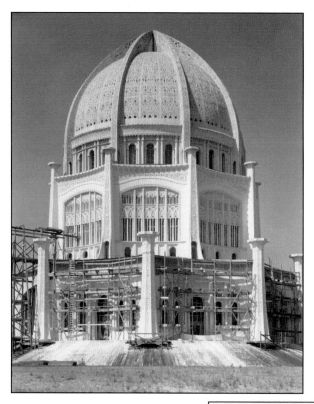

In May 1940, work could begin on the first three of the nine faces of the first story. Because of the different verses on each of the nine sides, nine different molds would be made. By summer, the nine main-story pylons were complete, and by the end of 1941, all nine sides were complete.

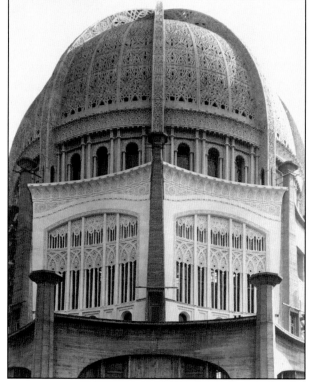

The color differences between the new decorative panels and the dome show the effects of the large dust storms of 1934. There were cleaning attempts in 1942, and chemicals and sandblasting were tried in the early 1970s. In the 1980s, an effective cleaning process was invented using only soap and water.

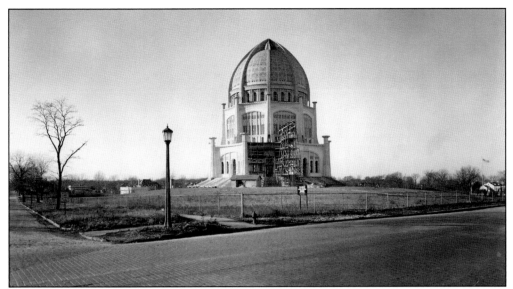

A photograph taken on December 18, 1941, from the corner of Linden Avenue and Sheridan Road shows the main story nearly complete. The final face has been cast, and all that is left to do is take down the scaffolding. The entire property is nearly 7 acres, and Linden Avenue is still paved with bricks today.

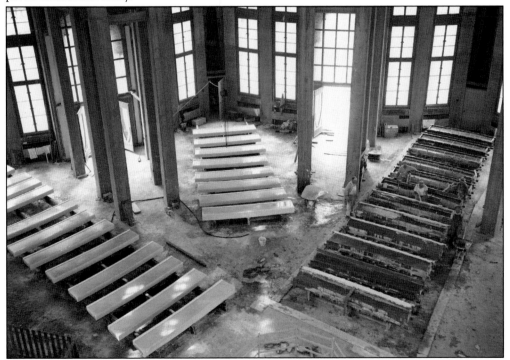

In 1942, the final contract for the Temple's exterior was signed for the 18 circular steps that would surround the building. With the steps being cast inside the auditorium, work began in May. It took a total of 972 sections (2 miles in length) and was one of the most expensive projects because of increased labor costs. On January 8, 1943, the exterior ornamentation was completed 17 months ahead of schedule.

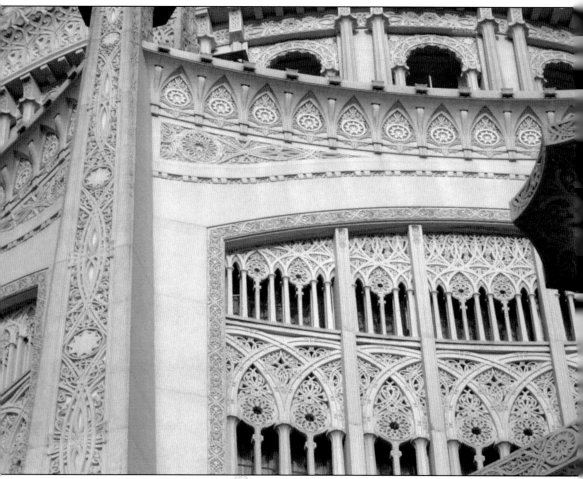

A close-up view of the panels on the gallery looking up to the clerestory shows elaborate decorations in details too small to take in from below. The craftsmanship, of both Louis Bourgeois and the sculptors of the Earley Studio, is evident in the little details. One could ask, "How many nine-pointed stars can you find in this picture?" (Courtesy of the Armbruster Company.)

Six

THE INTERIOR IS SET AGLOW

Architect Louis Bourgeois made artistic renderings for the design of the interior of the auditorium, but no specific decisions had been made before his death. His original plans called for stained glass, ornamental metal doors, small chapels or rooms representing the world's faiths, a solid dome, hundreds of lights, and a search light. When it came time to realize these plans, several practical problems remained to be solved, and some ideas came to be seen as unnecessarily elaborate and uncomfortably expensive. Several teams of architects and engineers worked together on creating simpler and more practical designs. Practical decisions also needed to be made for lighting, heating, ventilation, plumbing, and acoustics.

Chicago architect Alfred Shaw of Shaw, Metz, and Dolio prepared the final design plans, using the best of Bourgeois's "freedom of expression and graceful flow of lines." They were approved in May 1948. The George A. Fuller Company was hired to manage the construction, and the Earley Studio returned to create the interior in a more subtle white architectural concrete. A beautiful new staircase was built, and elegant glass and metal doors were installed.

Photographs of the interior of the Bahá'í Temple tend to focus on the beauty of the auditorium, the dome, and the sunlight streaming in on visitors in the midst of prayer and meditation. There are no decorative windows or works of art to distract from communion with God. Verses from the Bahá'í Writings are inscribed in each of the nine alcoves. They are from the Writings of Bahá'u'lláh and are the essential teachings of the Bahá'í Faith:

> All the Prophets of God proclaim the same faith.
> Religion is a radiant light and an impregnable stronghold.
> Ye are the fruits of one tree, and the leaves of one branch.
> So powerful is unity's light that it can illumine the whole earth.
> Consort with the followers of all religions with friendliness.
> O Son of Being! Thou are My lamp and My light is in thee.
> O Son of Being! Walk in My statutes for love of Me.
> Thy Paradise is My love; thy heavenly home is reunion with Me.
> The light of a good character surpasseth the light of the sun.

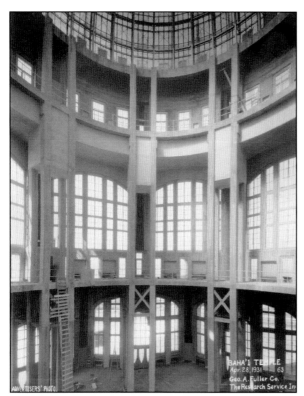

Shown is the interior of the Temple as it appeared in April 1931, which was around the time the outside construction was being completed. Very little was changed inside the interior for many years.

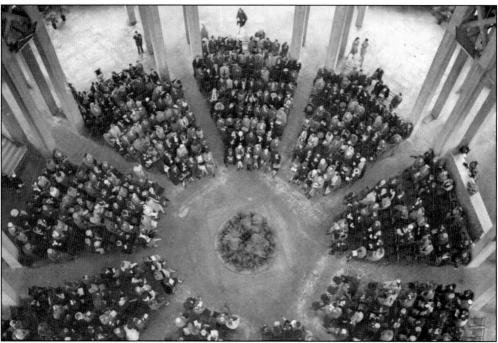

A devotional service meets in the unfinished auditorium in 1944, celebrating the centenary of the Bahá'í Faith. In the center are plants around the skylight that brought sunlight into Foundation Hall below.

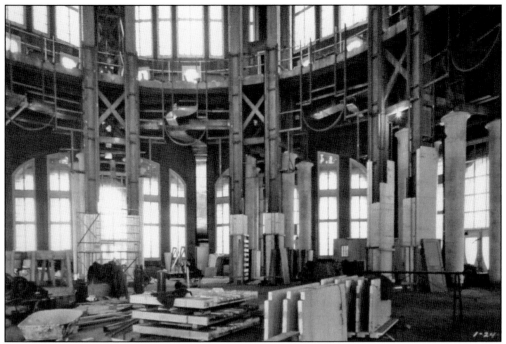

By January 1950, the transformation was underway. The square steel piers became white concrete tapered columns.

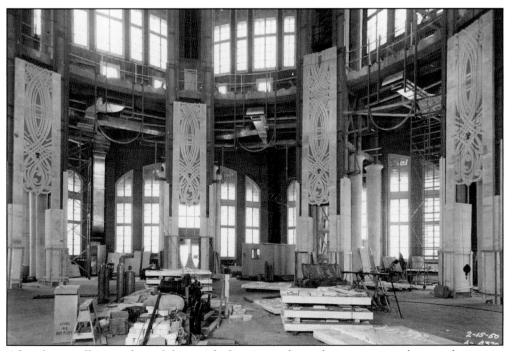

After the installation of metal ducting for heating and ventilation systems, alcove ceilings were built, and acoustical plaster was used in both the gallery and clerestory ceilings to reduce sound reverberation. A construction stairway was removed and a more beautiful one constructed.

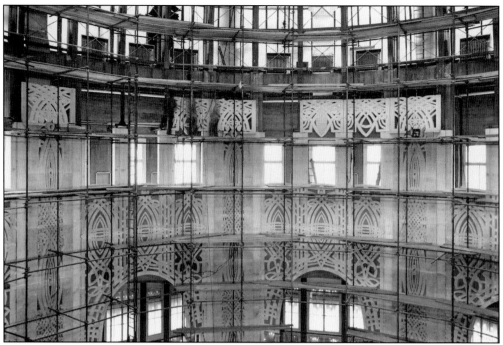

By September 1950, the ornamental panels had reached to the base of the dome. The three workmen in the center of the photograph are installing a panel nearly as tall as they are. Look closely to see the shadows of the ribs on the inside of the skylight.

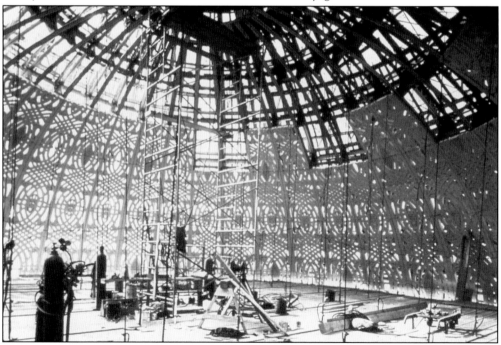

In February 1951, on a brilliant sunny day, a temporary floor has been constructed under the dome so that the ornamental panels can be attached to a steel frame built underneath the glass skylight.

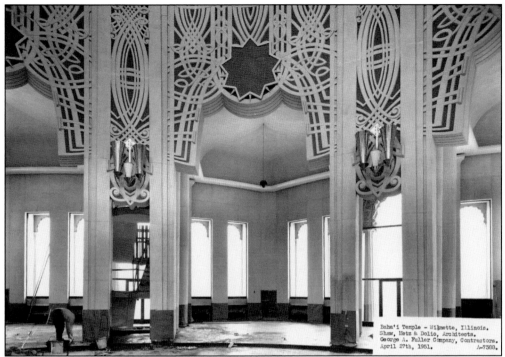

A workman makes preparations for the terrazzo floor to be installed. The beautiful shape of the alcove ceilings was created using two graceful ogee curves that join at the top. The nine-pointed star is a speaker for the sound system. The golden sconces shine light up to highlight the great curves and arcs drawn by Louis Bourgeois.

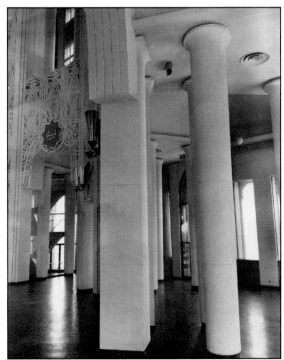

Once complete, the gleaming floors reflect the sunlight streaming from the dome and three levels of windows. On the far left, the new staircase can be seen. The "Greatest Name" calligraphy installed on the nine speakers was later removed.

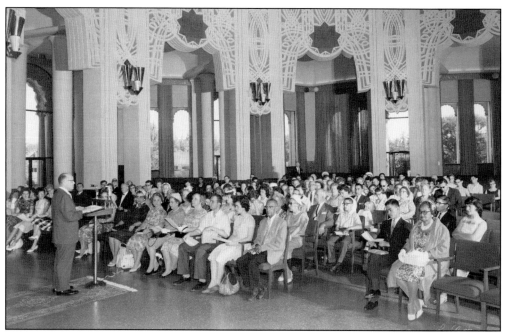

A devotional service from the 1960s shows how open the auditorium is to its environment; the lake, sky, and trees are all visible to those seated inside. When experienced in the summer, it can feel like the natural world outside is embracing the building. Curtains will later be installed against the dark for meetings at night and to reduce heat and glare on the gallery level.

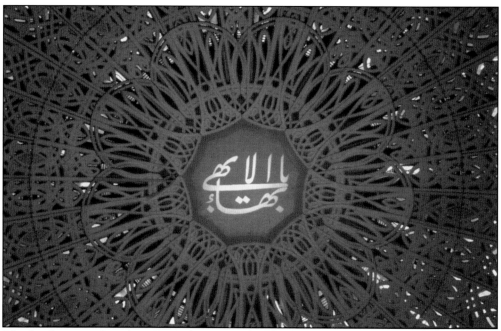

The finishing touch within the dome is the calligraphic rendering of the "Greatest Name" of God, "Yá Bahá'u'l-Abhá." It means, "O Glory of the Most Glorious" and is used in prayer and song and as an identifying symbol of the Bahá'í community.

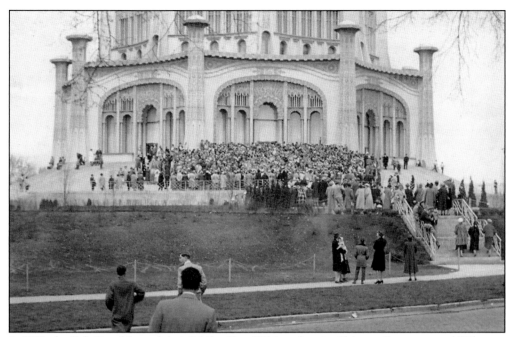

In 1953, the Bahá'ís celebrated their Jubilee Year. Taking place in Chicago, Evanston, and Wilmette were an international teaching conference, the national convention, and the formal dedication of the completed House of Worship, all scheduled for the same week in May. It was exactly 50 years since the meeting of Chicago's House of Spirituality first discussed the Mashriqu'l-Adhkár in Ashgabat and expressed a desire for one of their own.

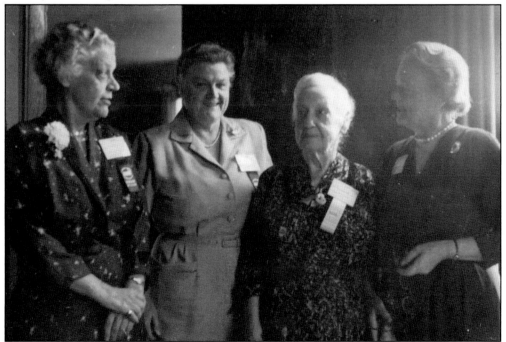

Age 91, and known throughout the Bahá'í world as the Mother of the Temple, Corinne True attended the dedication with her three daughters, Elizabeth, Arna, and Edna.

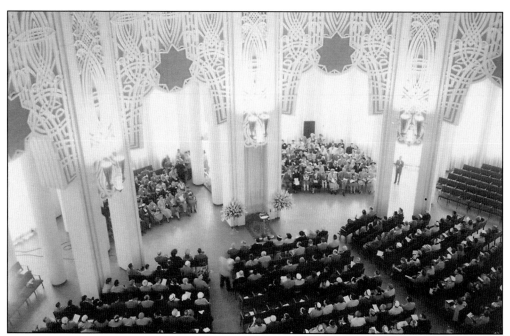

Four different devotional programs were held on the first weekend of May, each of them filling every chair in the auditorium, with hundreds of others turned away. Rúhíyyih Khánum, the wife of the head of the Bahá'í Faith, Shoghi Effendi, represented him at the dedication and read a message of greeting.

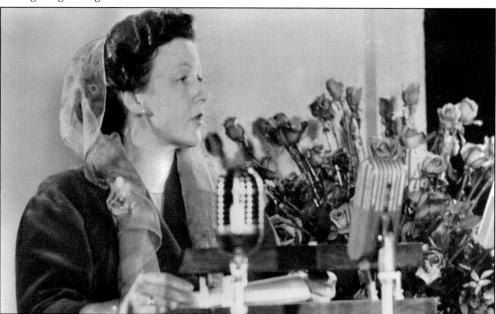

Rúhíyyih Khánum's parents, May Bolles and Sutherland Maxwell, were among the earliest Western Bahá'ís. She was born in New York City and raised in Montreal, Canada. Her father, an architect, was involved in the design and construction of several buildings at the Bahá'í World Center in Haifa, Israel. After the death of her husband in 1957, she traveled the world representing the Bahá'í Faith and participated at the dedications of future Houses of Worship.

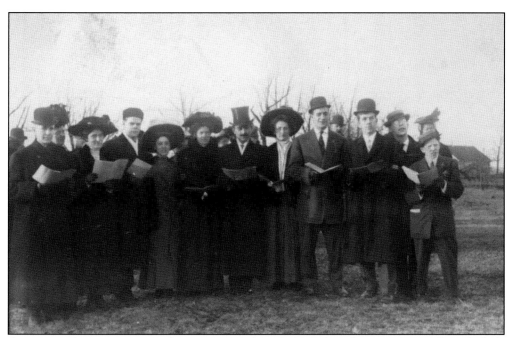

As soon as the property in Wilmette was purchased, the Bahá'ís began meeting there for holy days. This is the young folks' choir singing on March 21, 1909. The first day of spring is also the first day of the Bahá'í year, a holy day called Naw-Rúz, which is also celebrated at the beginning of the year by Zoroastrians and Persians. This would have been year 65 of the Bahá'í calendar, counting from 1844.

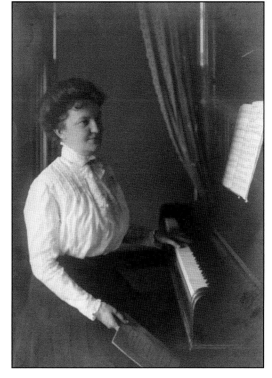

Louise R. Waite was called Shahnaz (Melody) by 'Abdu'l-Bahá in recognition of her many original verses and hymns. The early Chicago Bahá'ís were eager to develop their own musical identity. Songs and hymns were written about the Temple, and melodies were developed using Bahá'í prayers for lyrics. She wrote many hymns and songs of praise, and her "Temple Song" became extremely popular among the Bahá'ís.

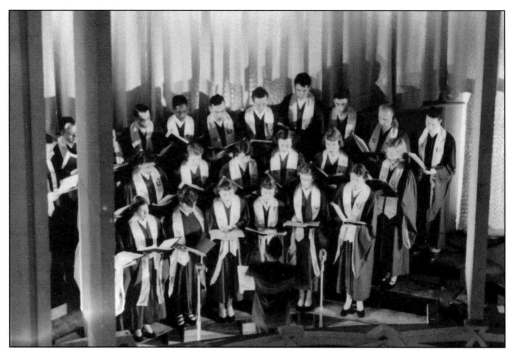

At the 1953 dedication, a choir from Northwestern University performed from the gallery at each of four services. The Bahá'í House of Worship Choir also often performs from this level during the Sunday afternoon devotionals and on holy days, but they do not wear robes.

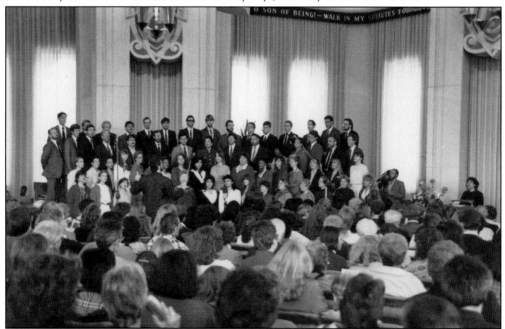

The House of Worship Choir, under the direction of Tom Price, sings in a 1992 devotional program commemorating the 100th anniversary of the passing of Bahá'u'lláh, the prophet-founder of the Bahá'í Faith. Music performed in the Temple auditorium uses only the human voice, in an attitude of prayer and devotion, with lyrics that are taken from the scriptures of the world's religions.

Seven

THE GARDENS BLOOM

The gardens surrounding the Bahá'í House of Worship are all one sacred space. They emphasize the beauty of the Temple and provide a natural setting for worship. Only from the gardens can the verses from the Bahá'í Writings inscribed on the nine faces of the first level of the Temple be seen. The tradition that Islamic mosques are decorated with verses from the Quran so greatly appealed to Louis Bourgeois that he included verses from the Bahá'í Writings in his plans. The selections used in the Temple design from the Writings of Baha'u'llah were chosen by Shoghi Effendi and could be said to represent the essence of Bahá'í teachings and belief:

> The earth is but one country, and mankind its citizens.
> The best beloved of all things in My sight is Justice;
> turn not away therefrom if thou desirest me.
> My love is My stronghold; he that entereth therein is safe and secure.
> Breathe not the sins of others so long as thou art thyself a sinner.
> Thy heart is My home; sanctify it for My descent.
> I have made death a messenger of joy to thee. Wherefore dost thou grieve?
> Make mention of Me on My earth, that in My heaven I may remember thee.
> O rich ones on earth! The poor in your midst are My trust; guard ye My trust.
> The source of all learning is the knowledge of God, exalted be His Glory.

With an intense focus on the construction of the Temple, the heavy equipment, and temporary buildings that were often required, the gardens were left until all else was complete. With nearly 5 acres of grounds to landscape and a requirement from 'Abdu'l-Bahá for nine gardens and nine fountains, it was one of those times for a master gardener to make "no little plans."

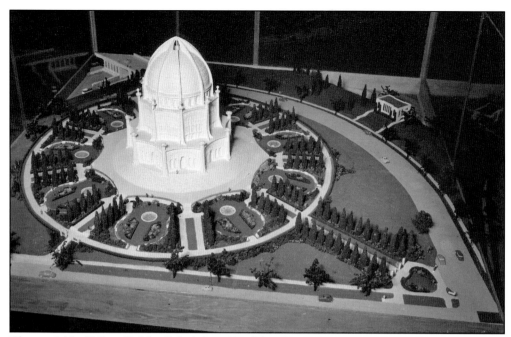

This model by Hilbert Dahl, a Bahá'í from Frankfort, Kentucky, proposes a circular terrace at the bottom of the monumental stairs that lead down to each garden with a stairway. The Chinese Junipers give the gardens a sense of quiet and privacy, while blocking noise from Sheridan Road. They also reflect the cypress trees planted in the Bahá'í properties in Israel.

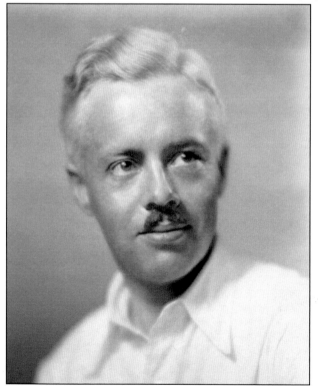

The design of the planting beds is consistent from garden to garden but allows for varied plantings in each. Dahl had been a guide at the Temple in the 1930s while living in Illinois and had begun drawings of gardens in 1938. His formal proposal was approved in July 1951.

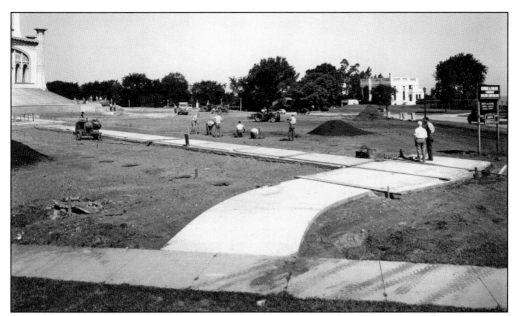

The George R. Fuller Company returned to construct the gardens in two stages. By the end of 1952, the terraces, stairs, walkways, many trees, and shrubs were installed. The lighting and the fountains were not installed until after the dedication in 1953.

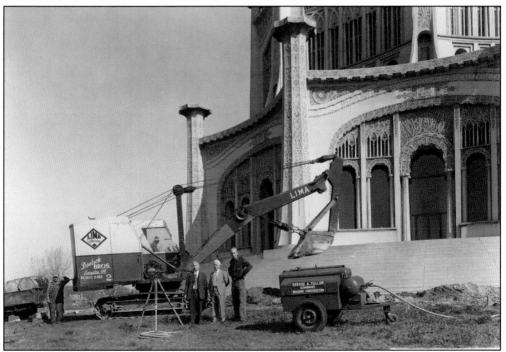

Berg and Dahl are listed as the landscape architects on the photograph above, but the five men in the picture are not identified. The driver of the excavator and his partner on the far left are surely from Doetsch Brothers in Evanston. Standing to the right of the machine, one of the other men might be the owner of the surveyor's equipment. The silver-haired man in the center looks to be Dahl.

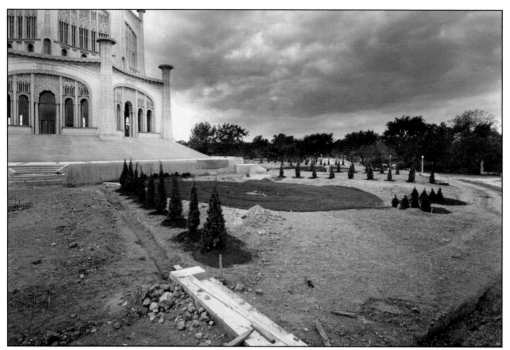

Lack of funds caused some aspects of the garden plan to remain incomplete. The most obvious feature missing from the finished gardens were the long curved concrete benches that embraced each garden and provided a restful place for prayer and meditation. Those took another 50 years until major renovations in 2006, for the benches to be constructed and installed in six of the restored gardens. The remaining three gardens will be completed in 2012.

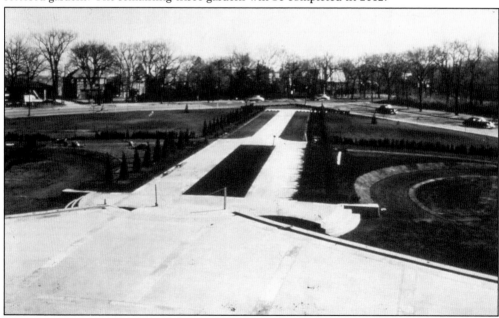

The "long approach" is the walkway that stretches all the way out to the corner of Sheridan Road and Linden Avenue. In future years, many beautiful flowering trees were planted at the corner to reflect the changing seasons and to absorb the sound from car traffic.

On March 6, 1953, L. Wyatt Cooper was hired to prepare the gardens for the dedication, which was scheduled to take place in six weeks. He tended those same gardens as the superintendent of buildings and grounds for the next 19 years until his retirement. He had a long association with the Bahá'í Faith, having been a member of Corinne True's children's classes in 1908.

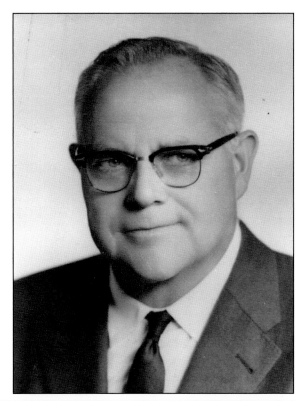

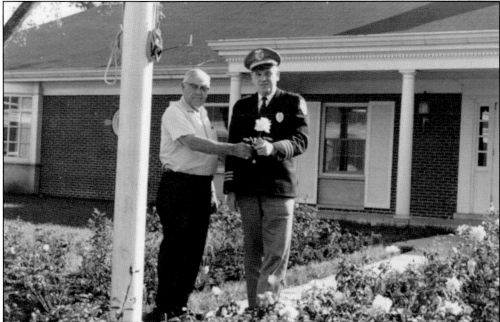

Wyatt Cooper participated in many garden organizations and societies, including the New Trier Men's Garden Club of the North Shore, the Men's Garden Club of America, and the American Rose Society. He helped the Village of Wilmette create rose gardens for both the police and fire stations. He is seen here in an undated photograph with chief of police Fred Stoecker.

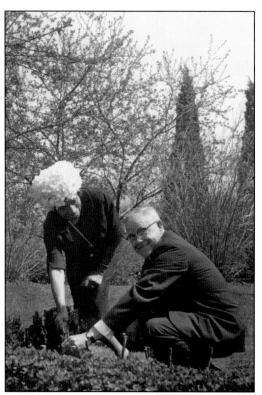

In 1962, the owners of Rose Hills Memorial Park near Los Angeles decided to name a rose for an outstanding African American to show at its next annual Pageant of Roses. A local Bahá'í associated with the park, F. Joseph McCormack suggested the contralto singer Marian Anderson. A cherry-red grandiflora with a "golden heart" was chosen, and with her permission, the American Rose Society registered it that year as the Marian Anderson Rose.

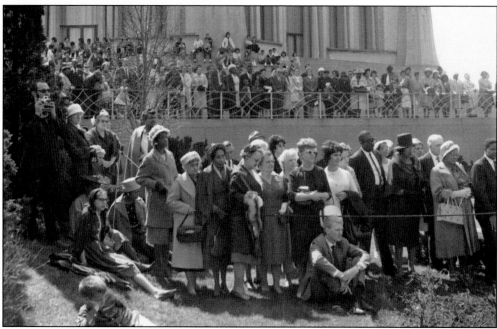

In 1964, the Bahá'ís requested the honor of planting a dozen roses in the Temple gardens in recognition of her "great talents, inspiration, and example to the people of America and the world." She agreed, and a date was set for May 3, 1964. Invitations for the event were sent to hundreds of local citizens "prominent in religious and civic affairs, the arts, and human rights."

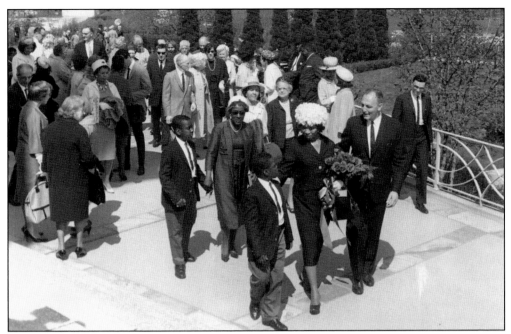

The event began at 2:30 with the arrival of Anderson. Dr. David S. Ruhe and Leroy Ioas escorted her into the gardens, and Jean Rankin of Glencoe, Illinois, presented her with a large bouquet of Marion Anderson roses shipped from California for the occasion. Wyatt Cooper was responsible for all the garden arrangements and assisted Anderson in planting one of the rosebushes.

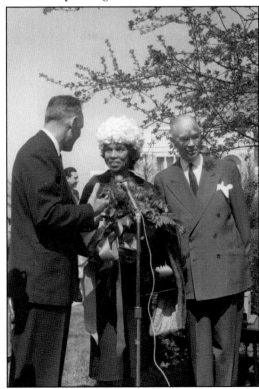

Also present were Howard C. Decker for the Village of Wilmette, Clarence C. Smith for the American Rose Society of Illinois and Indiana, and Jacob Barmore, consul-general of the State of Israel. After several short talks in the gardens and the planting one rosebush, a devotional program was held in the House of Worship, which was followed by a reception at 536 Sheridan Road.

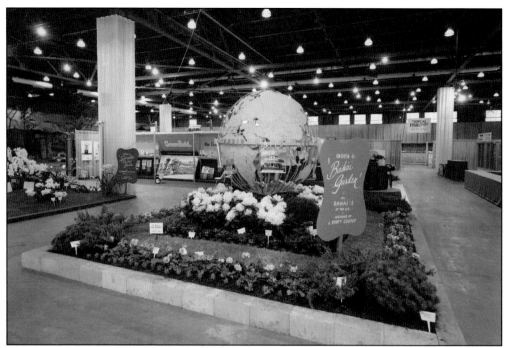

In the summer of 1962, officials of the annual Chicago World Flower and Garden Show requested an exhibit about the Temple to be included in the following spring's show at McCormick Place. Wyatt Cooper spearheaded this effort in consultation with Hilbert Dahl, the architect of the Temple gardens. The display garden measured 40 by 45 feet, nearly one-half the size of one of the actual gardens. It contained a pool, a fountain, grass, and several hundred flowering plants.

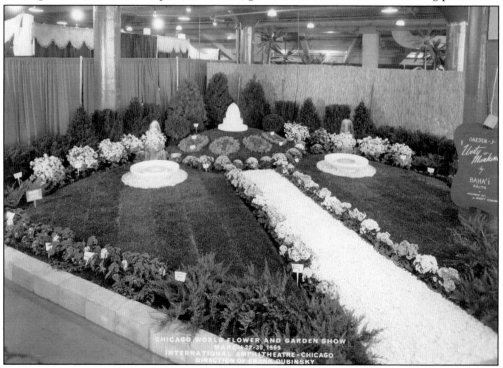

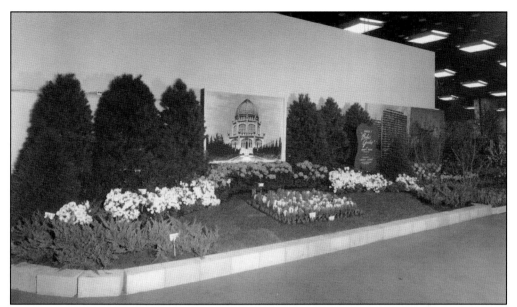

The Chicago World Flower and Garden Show was held at the McCormick Place in 1966, the World Amphitheater in 1967, and the International Amphitheatre in 1970. The show became a yearly tradition for the Bahá'ís, eventually involving thousands of volunteer hours contributed by members living close to the Temple. Although many were involved in the designing and building of the displays, most assisted in staffing an adjacent Bahá'í information booth. The Bahá'ís were involved with the show for nearly two decades, and several of their exhibits received awards.

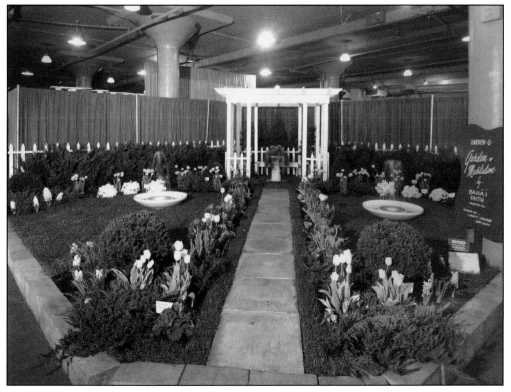

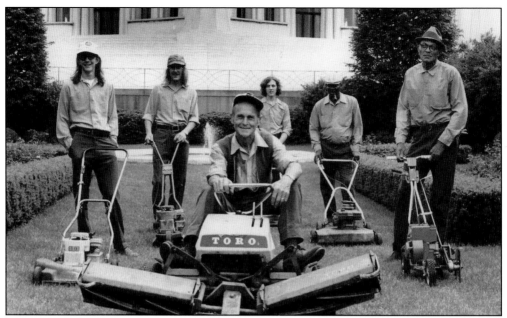

The grounds crew was often a mix of local students working for a summer and seasoned veterans who spent many years developing an intimate relationship with the building and year-round care of the gardens. In this 1970 photograph taken for a Bahá'í periodical, the crew displays the machines needed to do their work. From left to right, they are David Frye, Mark Harries, Paul Stirnemann, John ?, Adolph Estes, and Jim Edwards.

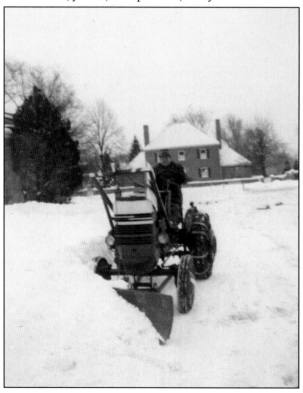

With a property that is open 365 days a year, snow removal in the winter is a priority. In an undated photograph, Wyatt Cooper is driving this unusual snowplow, which is just the right size for sidewalks and garden paths.

In 1970, new outdoor lighting was installed in the gardens to show off the Temple at night. In the summer, the Temple and gardens are open until 10:00 p.m.

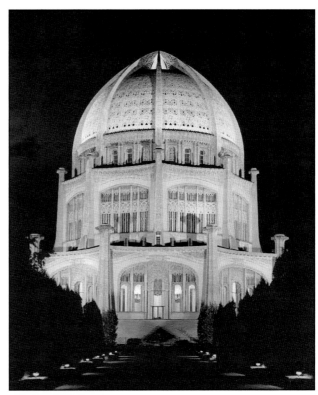

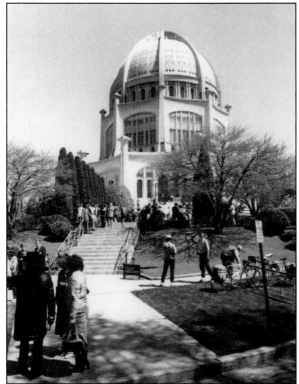

In Chicago-land, the House of Worship is a travel destination for tourists, school groups, international visitors, and even boaters tying up at the Wilmette Harbor. Sheridan Road is often busy with serious bicyclists who will visit the Temple to rest, get a drink of water, and gather a quiet thought in the gardens. The large pannier bags of these bicycle travelers suggest a serious outing.

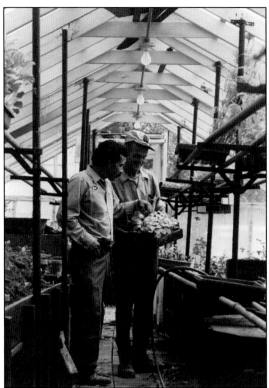

As the complexity of the gardens grew, it became convenient to grow many bedding plants on-site in a little greenhouse that can be seen just north of 110 Linden in aerial photographs. This allowed the gardeners to raise flowers that would not be commercially available locally. Ernie Lopez and Paul Stirnemann are showing particularly successful starts in this 1970s photograph.

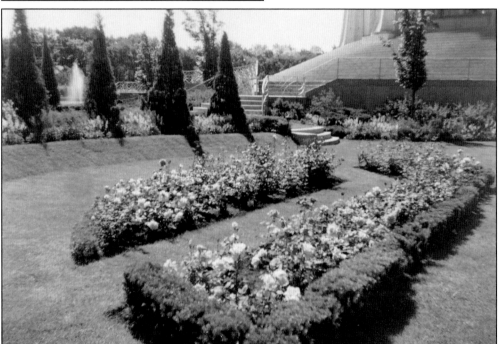

A promotional picture of the gardens shows well-tended planting beds, the Chinese Junipers, and flowering trees not yet at full height. The grassy slope is where the bench wall will be installed in later years.

Eight

THE TEMPLE IN
THE COMMUNITY

A letter from 'Abdu'l-Bahá explains the social network that will surround the central edifice of a Bahá'í House of Worship: "The Mashriqu'l-Adhkár is one of the most vital institutions in the world, and it hath many subsidiary branches. Although it is a House of Worship, it is also connected with a hospital, a drug dispensary, a traveler's hospice, a school for orphans, and a university for advanced studies. Every Mashriqu'l-Adhkár is connected with these five things. My hope is that the Mashriqu'l-Adhkár will now be established in America and that gradually the hospital, the school, the university, the dispensary, and the hospice—all functioning according to the most efficient and orderly procedures—will follow. Make these matters known to the beloved of the Lord, so that they will understand how very great is the importance of this 'Dawning-Point of the Remembrance of God.' The Temple is not only a place for worship; rather, in every respect is it complete and whole," according to *Selections from the Writings of 'Abdu'l-Bahá* pages 99 and 100.

Several colleges, hospitals, pharmacies, and schools do currently surround the Bahá'í properties in Evanston and Wilmette, but they arose independently to serve these communities. The Bahá'í Home for the Aged at 401 Greenleaf Avenue in Wilmette was opened in 1958 by the Bahá'ís as the first dependency of the House of Worship.

Chicago Bahá'ís traveled throughout the Midwest to teach their faith; Corinne True taught the first believers in Fruitport and Grand Rapids, Michigan. Kenosha, Wisconsin, is the second oldest Bahá'í community in the United States. Today there are Bahá'ís in every state and city, with large populations in Texas, South Carolina, and California. Before they attained statehood, the Bahá'ís in Hawaii and Alaska had elected their own National Spiritual Assemblies, and these remain as distinct institutions. Up until 1948, the National Spiritual Assembly represented the Bahá'ís of the United States and Canada, but in that year, each community elected its own governing body.

The Bahá'í House of Worship in Wilmette, beloved by believers throughout the world, is known as the "Mother Temple of the West." At present, there are Bahá'í Houses of Worship on every continent: Kampala, Uganda; Sydney, Australia; Frankfurt, Germany; Panama City, Panama; New Delhi, India; and Apia, Western Samoa, with another under construction in Santiago, Chile. Eventually, every Bahá'í community will have its own Mashriqu'l-Adhkár, a place of prayer and meditation open to everyone.

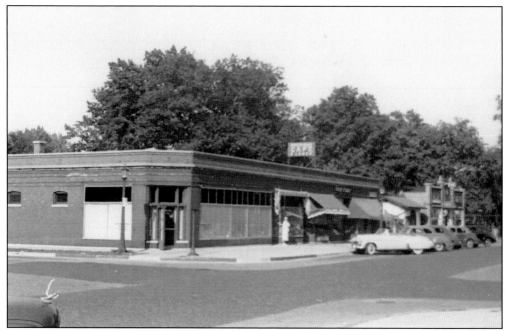

The nearest commercial center to the House of Worship is at Fourth Street and Linden Avenue in Wilmette. The Chicago Transit Authority's Linden Station is the final stop on today's Purple Line. This photograph from 1949 shows businesses across the street from the train station on Linden, including the Sheridan Cafe and Lunch. (Courtesy of the Wilmette Public Library.)

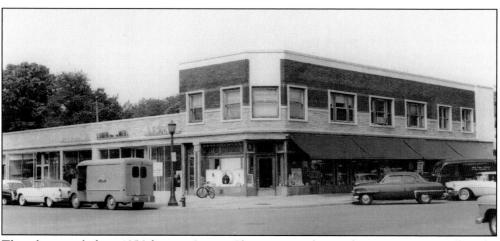

This photograph from 1956 features Lyman Pharmacy on the northwest corner, as well as the Linden Store for Men and the Wests Sports Shop to the left. This business district is also known as Linden Square. (Courtesy of the Wilmette Public Library.)

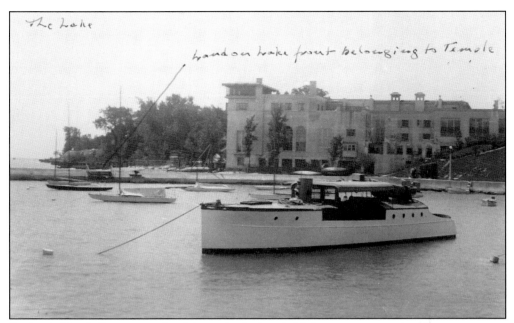

Benjamin Marshall was a noted architect who had made his fortune constructing luxury apartment buildings in Chicago. In 1921, he spent more than $1 million on his Wilmette lakeside mansion, including a glassed-in tropical garden and a 5th-century Chinese temple. In 1936, Nathan Goldblatt purchased the mansion and later offered it to the Village of Wilmette as a gift when taxes on it became too high.

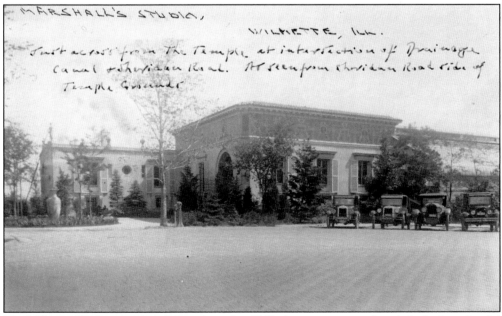

The Village of Wilmette refused the gift, and in 1950, the mansion was demolished after a fire did extensive damage. The Bahá'ís purchased the 2.6 acres of land, which currently serves as an overflow parking lot and staging area for the restoration project's construction materials. All that's left of the Marshall mansion are lovely ornamental iron gates on the driveway off Sheridan Road.

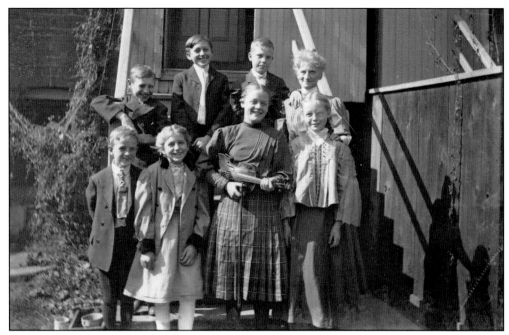

Dr. Susan Moody taught the first Chicago children's classes, which must have been delightful from the looks on the faces of these youngsters in this October 14, 1906, photograph The following are (first row), from left to right, John Gale, Lilyn "Lillie" Walters, Katherine True, and Christina Peterson; (second row) Edward Gale, Ernest Walters, Chester Rasmussen, and Susan I. Moody.

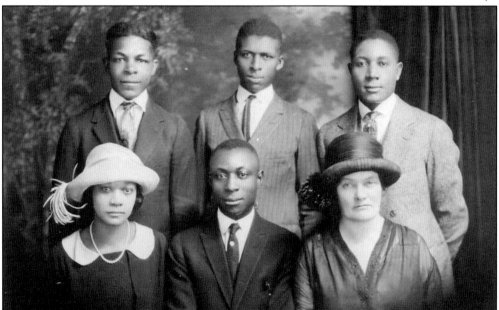

From its earliest days, there were active and involved African American members of the Chicago Bahá'í community. The following are, from left to right: (first row, seated) Vivian Wesson, unidentified, and Kakab MacCutean; (second row, standing) Ira Hightower, Irving Johnson, and Henry Wesson. Vivian Wesson was Corinne True's cook for two years and traveled to Togo, West Africa, in 1954 as a Bahá'í teacher.

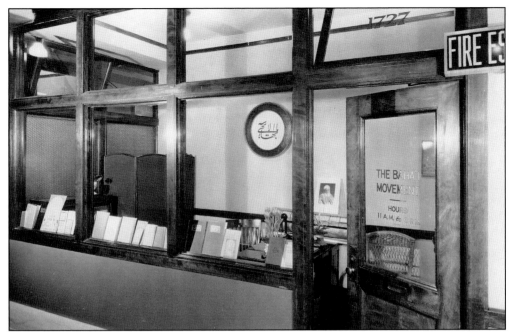

In 1930, Ida B. Slaton wrote a report about the Chicago Bahá'í Headquarters (perhaps the first office of its kind), room 1727 in the Stevens Building at 14 North State Street in Chicago. It was opened on January 2, 1929, and staffed from 11:00 a.m. to 3:00 p.m. every day but Sunday. Books and pamphlets were available for purchase. The sign refers to the "Bahá'í Movement," a term often used at the time.

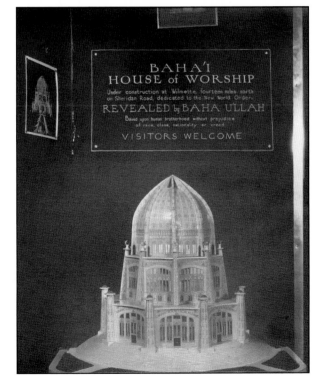

Made by Louis Voelz of Kenosha, Wisconsin, this small model of the Temple was on display at the Hall of Religions during the 1933 Chicago's Century of Progress Exposition. As a result, many visitors traveled north to Wilmette to attend lectures and watch the delivery of the first ornamental concrete panels.

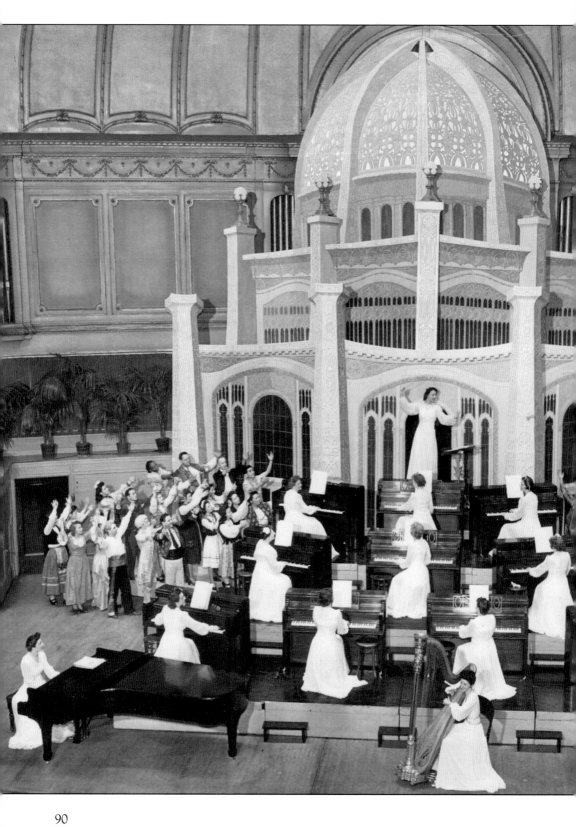

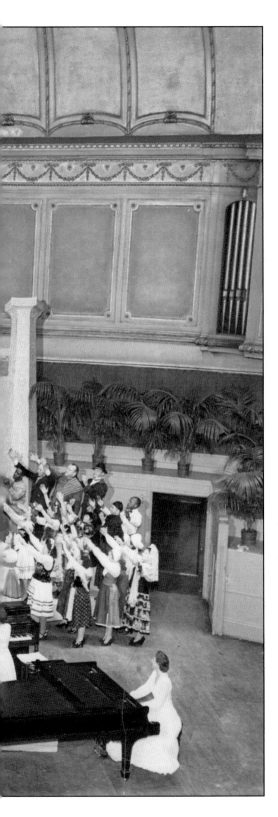

The reverse of this wonderful photograph explains that this was a performance in Chicago's Orchestra Hall by the Ladies Piano Symphony. How this musical work was written and performed has not been well remembered by the Baháʼís. The proportions of the Temple set piece are not quite accurate, and it shows the lanterns that never were. On the back, the following is written: "The Chicago 'Grand Ladies' Piano Symphony Orchestra on Wednesday, May 24 at Orchestra Hall, Chicago. The new chorus, 'The Voices of All Nations,' sing the new music, 'The Making of the Temple,' with Antoinette Rich conducting." A close look at the costuming suggests those used by an opera chorus, but another close look reveals singers of all races, which was an exception for Chicago in the 1930s.

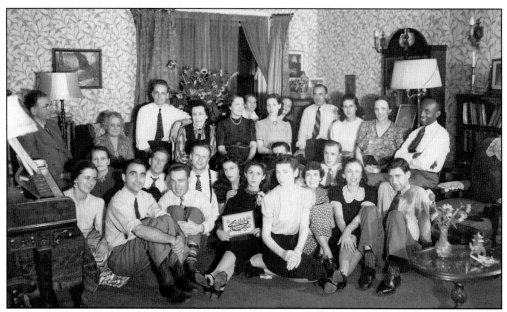

This 1940 Bahá'í fireside was held at the home of Lillian Dobbins in Chicago at 1669 Farwell Avenue. A fireside would begin with prayers and then a presentation by a noted speaker. Ellsworth Blackwell, the African American man on the far right, is perhaps the speaker at this fireside. He was a much-loved prominent Chicago Bahá'í. Hospitality was important, with plenty of sweet treats and pots of steaming tea, a tradition from the earliest days in Persia.

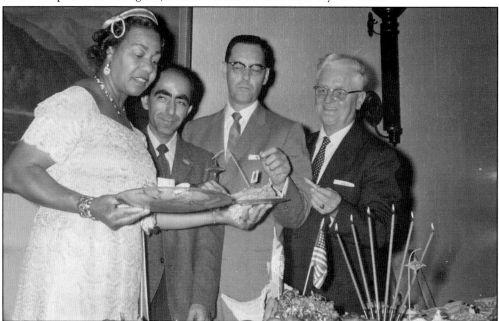

In commemoration of the Birth of the Báb, the prophet-herald of the Bahá'í Faith, a party was held on October 20, 1957, at the Fine Arts Building of Chicago, which was located at 410 South Michigan Avenue. Pictured are, from left to right, Kathelynea Kellum, Dr. Abbas Kessel, Laurence La Rocque, and Lloyd Robinson. Kathelynea and her husband, David Kellum (an editor at the *Chicago Defender*), were longtime active members of the Chicago Bahá'í community.

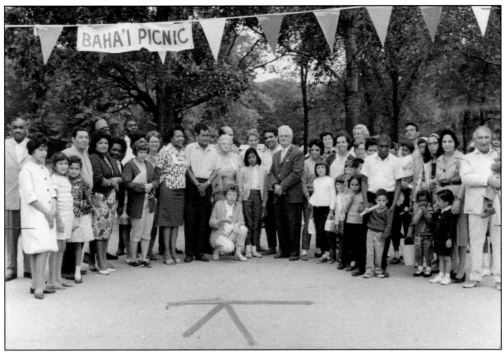

A Chicago Bahá'í picnic in August 9, 1964, gives believers of all ages a chance to gather together, play games, and share a meal.

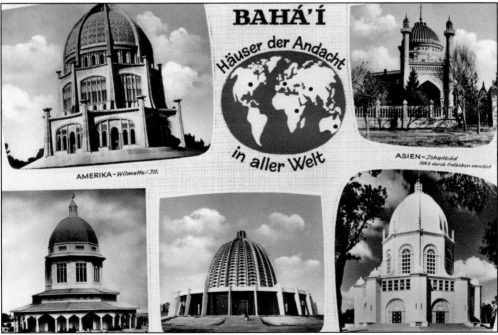

The postcard in German shows the "Hauser der Andacht in aller Welt," with dots on the map for the United States, Turkmenistan, Uganda, Germany, and Australia. The German Bahá'í House of Worship near Frankfort was dedicated July 4, 1964, and also has a home for the aged as a dependency.

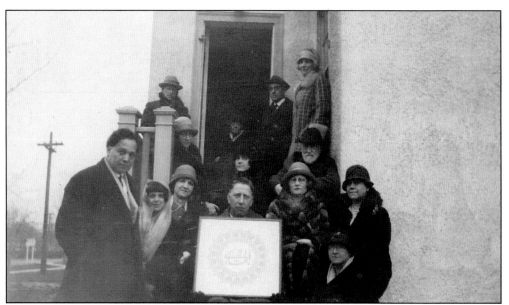

The first Spiritual Assembly of Wilmette was elected in 1927. This photograph was taken on the porch of 112 Linden Avenue, which was built to be the home of the property's caretaker, Alfred Anderson. Louis Bourgeois is sitting in the far back left. Standing at the far left is Dr. Zia Bagdadi who moved to Wilmette with his wife, Zeenat, in 1921. By 1937, there were 22 adult believers in the Wilmette Bahá'í community.

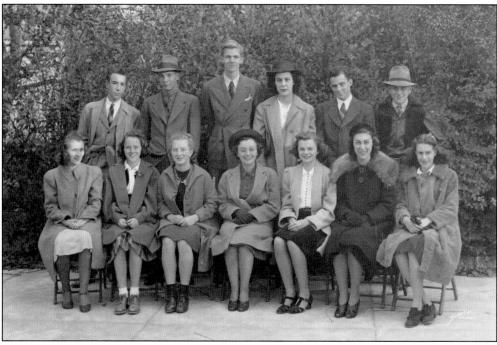

The Wilmette youth posed for a picture around 1938. The following are, from left to right: (first row, seated) Beatrice Tyler, Barbara Hannen, Zerah Lapp, Zamekal Morton, ? Morton, unidentified, and Cynthia Hastings; (second row, standing) Harlan Scheffler, two unidentified, Betty Scheffler, Sohail Hannen, and unidentified.

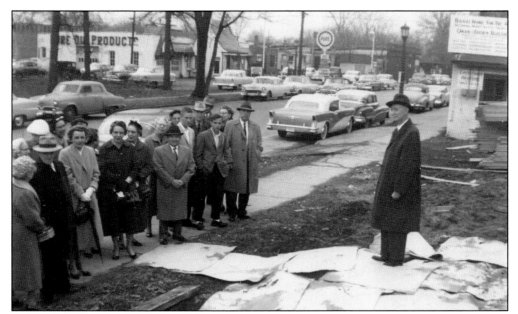

In this 1958 photograph, Horace Holley dedicated the Bahá'í Home for the Aged at 401 Greenleaf Avenue in Wilmette. He was the secretary of the National Spiritual Assembly from 1924 to 1959. Horace Holley had a career in New York advertising before moving to Wilmette and was a poet, author, playwright, and editor for many Bahá'í publications. Across the street is the distinctive Pure Oil gas station.

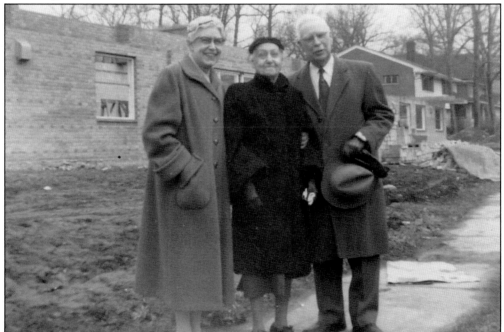

Sophie Loeding, Corinne True, and Carl Sheffler attended the dedication. Sophie Loeding was the first full-time employee of the Bahá'í Secretariat as Horace Holley's secretary. Years later she was a resident at the Bahá'í Home. Scheffler was a notable local artist and teacher and painted WPA murals that can still be seen in Evanston schools.

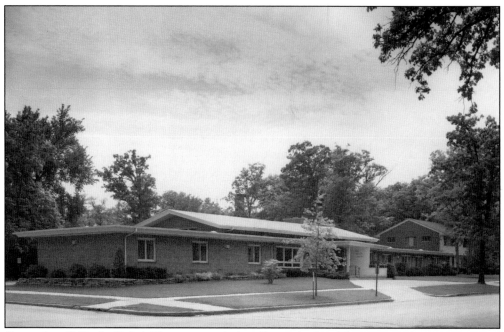

Opened in 1959, the Bahá'í Home was a sheltered care facility. There were administrators and a nurse on staff, but no significant medical care was provided. A kitchen staff served meals and afternoon tea. Programming for the residents included lectures, clubs, crafts, outings, and holiday events.

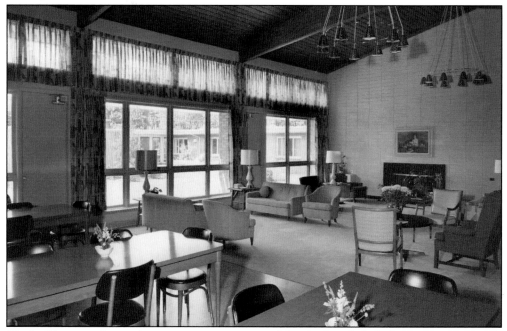

The building was designed to encourage community life, which included a large open space with a piano, library, a private patio garden, and a fireplace. The home was promoted throughout Wilmette and the North Shore as a facility open to people of all races and faiths, and there were never more than one or two Bahá'í residents at a time.

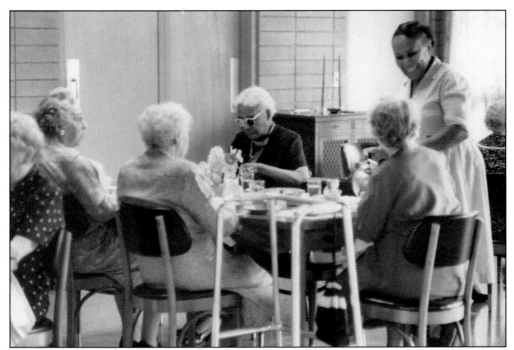

A Bahá'í Home brochure reads the following: "With continuous service to provide the aging of all races and religions with a home where they can live in dignity, freedom, and comfort, while their particular needs are lovingly and expertly cared for."

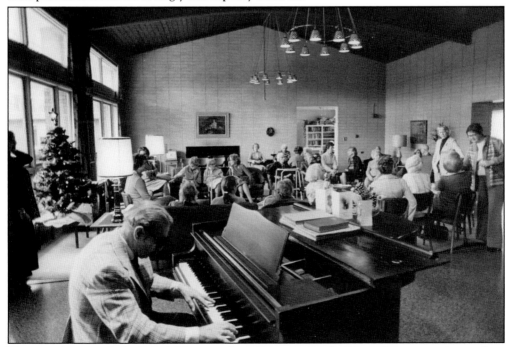

Time caught up with the Bahá'í Home in the 1990s, with the facility no longer meeting modern standards. It was closed in 2001 after 43 years of service. The building remains in use by the Bahá'ís of Wilmette for study groups, children's programs, and holiday gatherings.

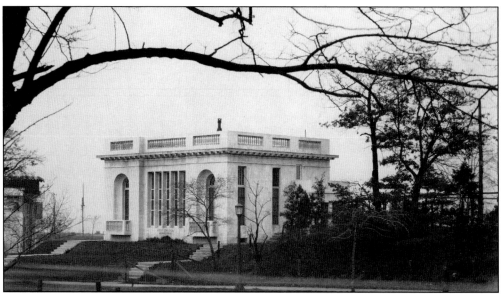

In this undated photograph, a small sign on the front of 536 Sheridan advertises Louis Bourgeois Architect. After his death, the studio was purchased from his wife, Alice, and the building was remodeled into a modern home and meeting place for the National Spiritual Assembly. Built from scrap lumber left over from Temple construction, by 1985, it was determined that it could not be preserved and instead should be replaced.

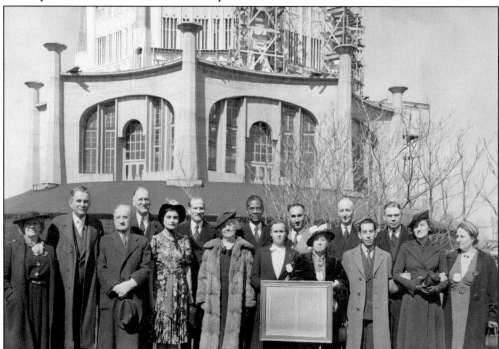

The nine members of the National Spiritual Assembly live throughout the United States and are elected for a one-year term. They meet together about once a month, most often in Wilmette, but sometimes at other locations. This meeting in the 1940s was with visitors from Central and South America.

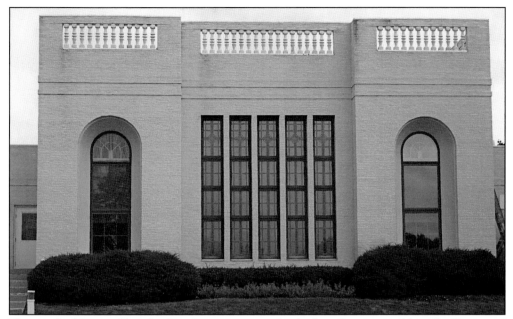

The new building on Sheridan Road was constructed to look as close as possible to the Bourgeois' home. As the seat of the National Spiritual Assembly and its formal address, it represents the Bahá'í institution of the Hazíratu'l-Quds, which is Arabic and means "the Sacred Fold." Its component parts are called today the Bahá'í National Center, which include the secretariat, treasury, archives, a library, and publishing office.

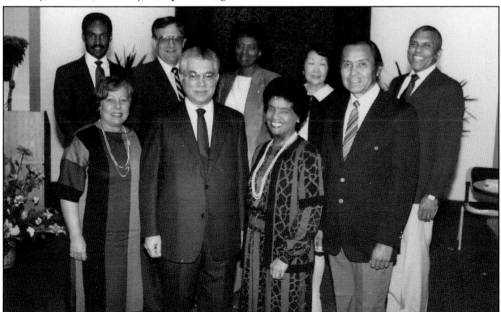

In 1985, the members of the National Spiritual Assembly were, from left to right, Robert C. Henderson, Dorothy Nelson, James Nelson, Firuz Kazemzadeh, Alberta Deas, Wilma Brady, Soo Fouts, Chester Kahn, and William C. Maxwell. The National Spiritual Assembly is elected at an annual convention with 171 delegates from the contiguous 48 states. Every adult Bahá'í, age 21 or over, is eligible for election.

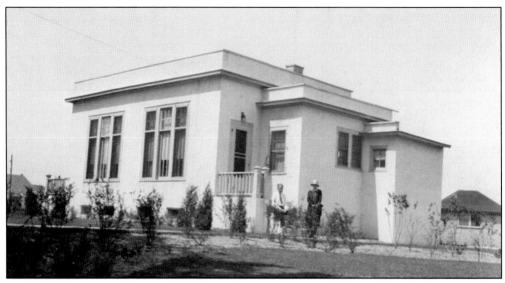

In 1948, the caretaker's home at 112 Linden Avenue was remodeled as offices for the secretariat, treasury, and publishing. Soon an addition was required, and then a smaller building at 110 was built for the Publishing Trust. After the majority of offices moved to 1233 Central Street in Evanston, these became offices and workrooms for properties and grounds and later the home of the Temple Conservation Library.

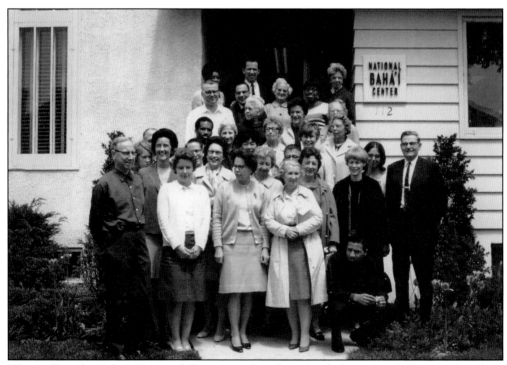

The staff at the Bahá'í National Center in this photograph from the 1960s would include accountants, secretaries, editors, and mail-room clerks.

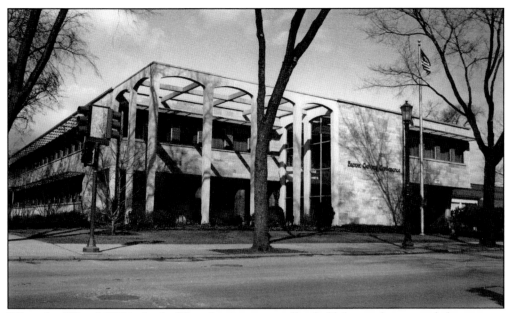

When the 110 and 112 Linden buildings became too small to hold the employees needed to manage the activities of the American Bahá'ís, several other small offices in Evanston and Wilmette were rented. In 1980, this handsome building at 1233 Central Street in Evanston was purchased, and nearly all of the departments were combined into one National Center.

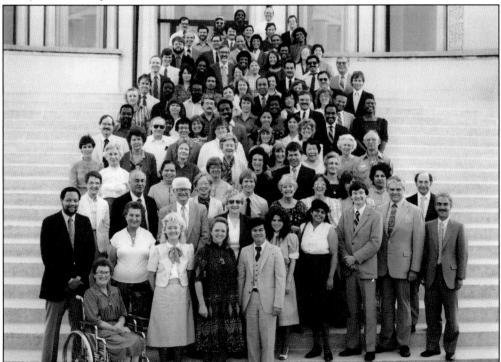

In a long tradition of photographs taken on these steps, the 1985 staff and visiting national committees posed together. Not every employee at the National Center is expected to be a member of the Bahá'í Faith.

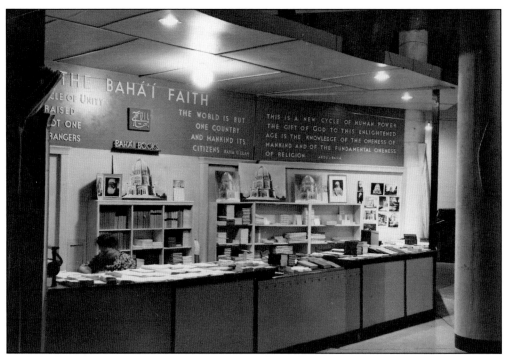

The visitor's center tucked away within the building's foundation has welcomed tourists since 1932. It has always featured a bookstore with a display of titles about the history and belief of the Bahá'í Faith, including prayer books, postcards, jewelry, and teaching materials.

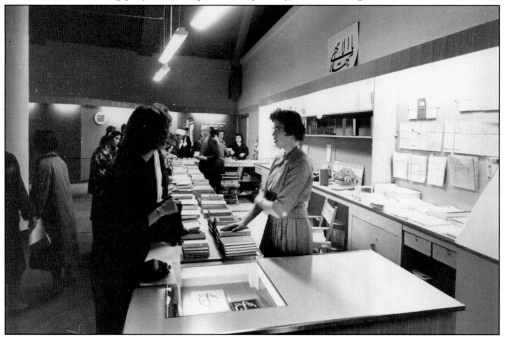

This undated photograph shows an expanded bookstall and office. Well-trained volunteers who know current (and out-of-print) inventory staff the bookstore. A supply of Bahá'í materials in a variety of languages was considered essential as tourists often visited the Temple from other nations.

In the 1970s, a small building was purchased at 415 Linden Avenue to be the home of Bahá'í Publishing. It is a regular stop on tours taken by National Convention delegates or those attending Special Visit programs at the House of Worship. The Bahá'í Publishing Trust and Distribution Service carries thousands of titles from Bahá'í publishers all over the world.

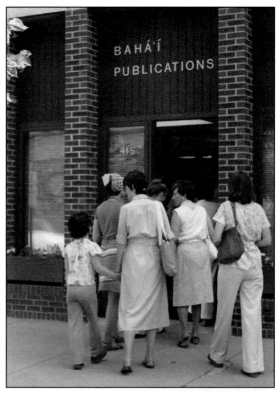

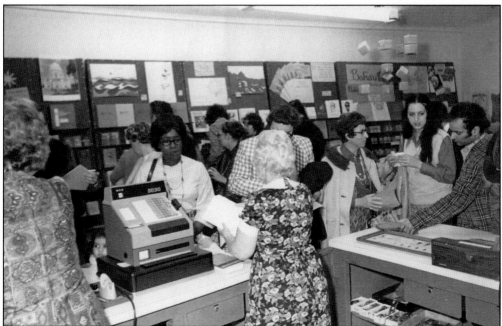

Pictured is a busy bookstore during National Convention in 1973. This was the time when visiting delegates could purchase everything new that year to display at reports throughout the United States. The sweet lady at the cash register is longtime volunteer Bea Somerhalder, and she can be seen as a teenager on page 94.

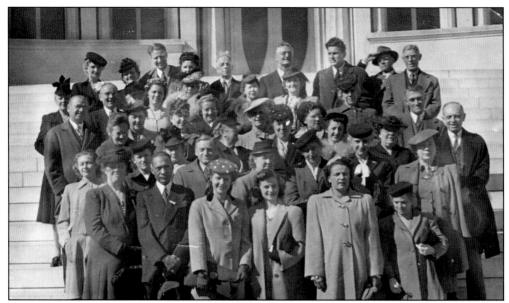

Pictured is the meeting of the Temple Guides Committee with some of the local area guides on October 15, 1944. The guides are from Chicago, Evanston, and Wilmette as well as from Kenosha, Racine, Milwaukee, Shorewood, and Bristol, Wisconsin.

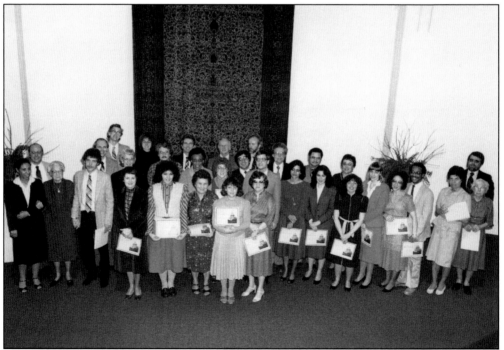

In honor of the many volunteer hours donated to the Temple, Corinne True Awards for Meritorious Service were presented annually from 1979. In 1983, certificates were given for guiding, choir, special events, Persian devotions, hospitality, dawn devotions, and youth guides. The Joliet Bahá'í community won an award for community guiding. On the far left, Ouida Coley of the activities staff is arm in arm with Edna True.

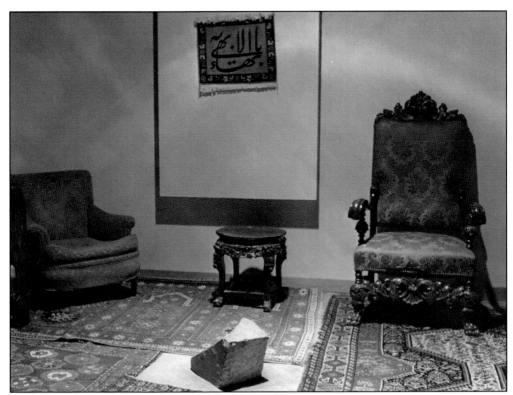

Nettie Tobin's stone never was a cornerstone. It was put in safekeeping when the foundations were dug and the foundation building was constructed. Small rooms have been built around it as the visitor's center has been remodeled several times. In 2010, a new exhibit will feature the stone to tell the story of the Temple's early history.

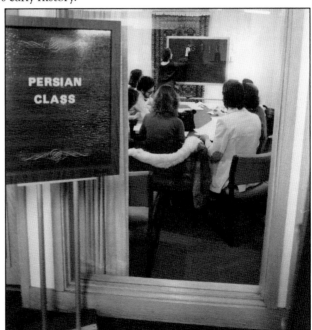

Numerous classes and lectures have been presented at the Temple over the years. After the 1978 revolution in Iran, many Persian Bahá'ís immigrated to the United States. Bahá'í communities often found themselves with new Persian families practically overnight, and there arose an interest in learning conversational Persian, hence this class in the visitor's center.

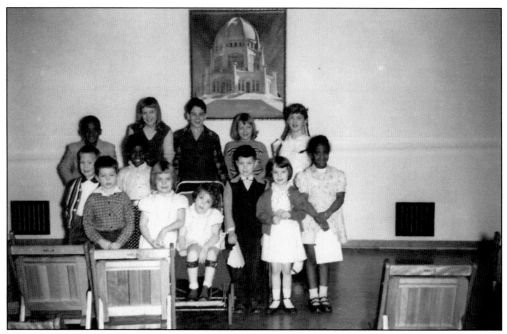

This children's class from the 1960s would have memorized prayers, learned a song, told stories, performed a play, or made a craft. Children's programs are scheduled regularly throughout the year, often to commemorate a Bahá'í holy day.

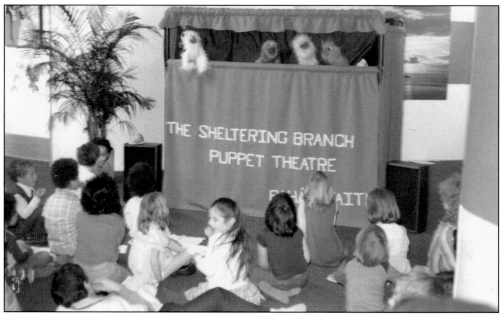

The Sheltering Branch Puppet Theatre has entertained children during holy day events on many different occasions over the years. Plays and stories would emphasize virtues such as kindness, generosity, humility, and forgiveness. This 1982 performance is during Ayyám-i-Há, which is several days at the end of February given over especially for celebration, charity, hospitality, and gift-giving.

National Convention delegate Van Gilmer performs in the 1980s in front of the exceptional Persian carpet that hung in Foundation Hall for many years. Instrumental music is welcome in Foundation Hall, which has hosted many choirs and musical groups. Gilmer is a composer, performer, and the current director of the Bahá'í House of Worship Choir.

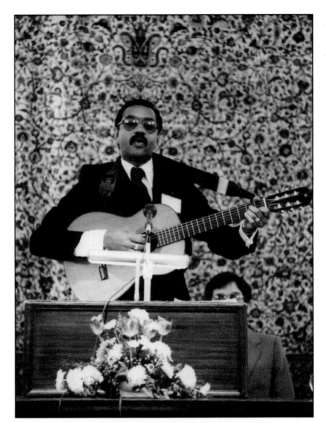

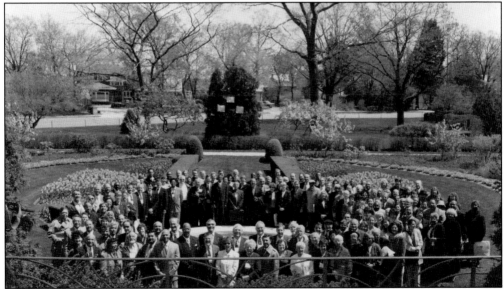

With the tulips in full bloom, the formal photograph of the 91st National Convention is taken in the gardens in 2000. National Conventions are counted from 1909, when Bahá'í Temple Unity first met in Chicago to consult about raising funds to purchase land for a Temple. Delegates representing districts throughout the continental United States elect the nine members of the National Spiritual Assembly.

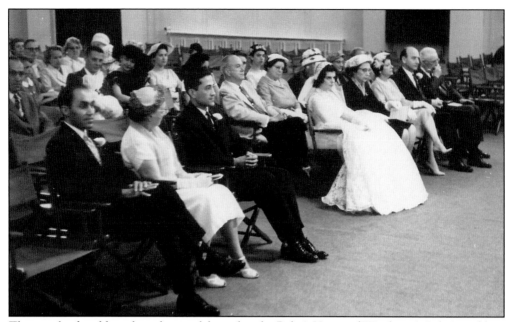

Thousands of weddings have been celebrated at the Bahá'í House of Worship. A Bahá'í wedding is simple, with only one vow said by the bride and groom, which is, "We will all, verily, abide by the Will of God." As there is no clergy in the Bahá'í Faith, the couple may ask anyone they choose to read from a selection of prayers, blessings, or poetry that they make themselves. (Courtesy of the Khavari family.)

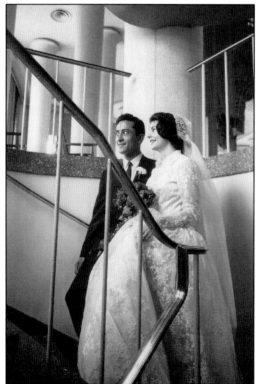

The official for the wedding is a member or representative of a Bahá'í local Spiritual Assembly. All states in the United States authorize Bahá'í Assemblies to officiate weddings. On any given weekend in the summer, wedding parties from throughout the North Shore will stop at the Temple gardens for photographs, but only Bahá'í weddings may take place at the Bahá'í House of Worship. (Courtesy of the Khavari family.)

Sue and Khalil Khavari of Menlo Park, California, were married in Wilmette on June 6, 1959. Their ceremony was held in Foundation Hall with friends and family, and afterwards they walked up the inside stairwell to say prayers together in the auditorium. (Courtesy of the Khavari family.)

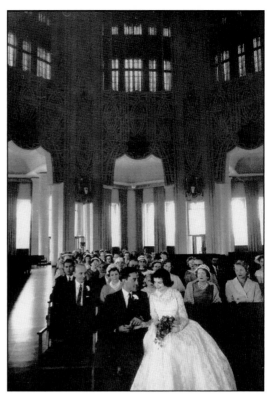

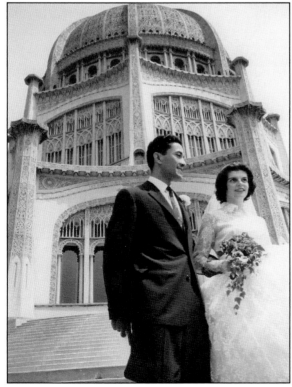

Weddings may also be held in the gardens, but receptions or meals are held elsewhere. The Khavaris celebrated their 50th anniversary in 2009 and have six grandchildren. (Courtesy of the Khavari family.)

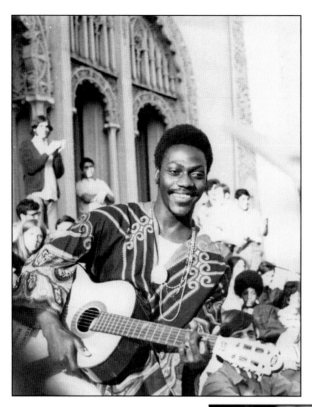

Bahá'í youth have a distinctive station within their faith. Between reaching the age of spiritual maturity at 15 and participation in Bahá'í elections at age 21, they are encouraged to teach, travel, gain education and career skills, and enjoy the energy and activity that comes naturally to them.

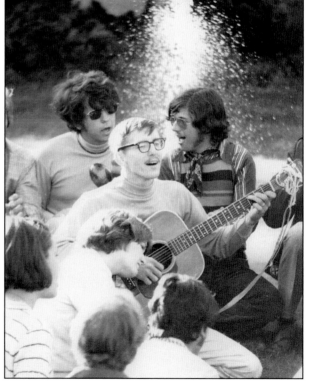

In 1970, Bahá'í youth conferences were held throughout the world, including more than 2,000 youth from every state and more than 20 nations who met in June at Evanston Township High School. The Bahá'ís of Wilmette sponsored a music festival that included a performance by Seals and Crofts, Wednesday's Children, and anyone else who had a guitar.

These youth cheerfully express the value Bahá'ís place on racial diversity. With a core belief in the oneness of humanity and the elimination of prejudice, interracial marriage is celebrated within the Bahá'í Faith, as well as a commitment to address racism as its most challenging issue.

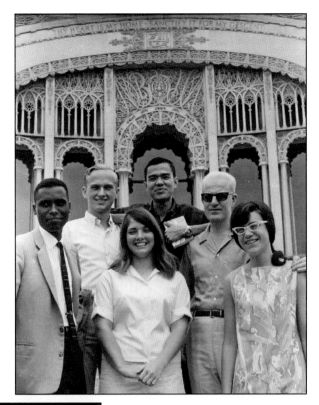

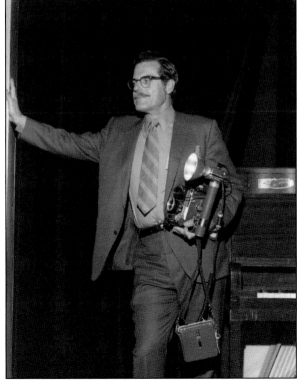

Many of the photographs in this book were taken by Kenneth Jennrich, a longtime member of the Wilmette Bahá'í community and a professional photographer. He was captured on film, along with his sophisticated camera, at the 1970 youth conference.

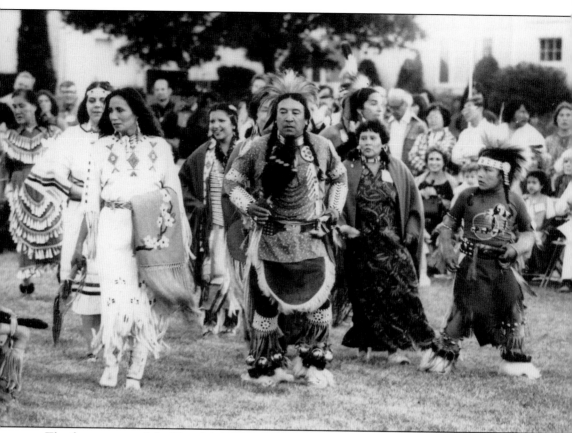

The first owners of the Temple's lakeshore property were Archange and Antoine Ouilmette. Archange and her children were members of the local Potawatomi tribe. They settled here for many years; their home open to travelers passing through. Their property was sold over time to the Village of Wilmette, which is named for this family. In 1980, an Intertribal Bahá'í Council was called, inviting Native American Bahá'ís from Canada, Alaska, and the continental United States, to gather for a conference held at the National College of Education in Evanston. During the conference, several films about Native American history and culture were shown in Foundation Hall along with displays of cultural exhibits. The closing powwow was held on the property behind 536 Sheridan Road.

A featured dancer in 1980, Kevin Locke is a prominent Lakota Sioux musician and hoop dancer. He currently leads a dance troupe that travels as cultural ambassadors for the United States throughout the world. He has performed in 70 countries over 30 years, most recently at the 2009 Parliament of World Religions in Melbourne, Australia.

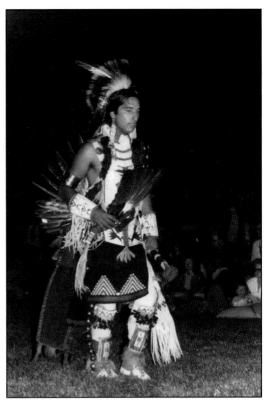

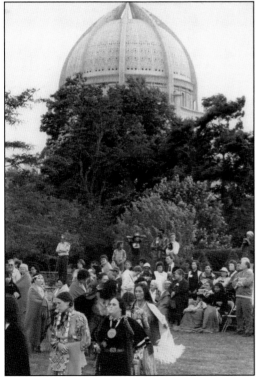

Cultural diversity is highly valued in the Bahá'í Faith. There are more than 2,000 ethnic groups represented in the worldwide Bahá'í community, and Bahá'í prayers have been translated into more than 800 languages. Indigenous Bahá'í communities have participated in cultural exchanges throughout Central and South America, the Arctic, and throughout Northern Europe and Siberia.

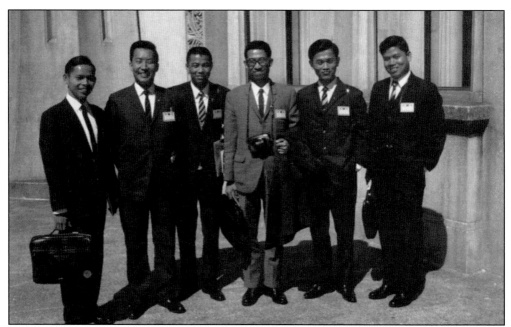

This visiting group from Taiwan in the 1960s was part of a Rotary Club exchange program. From its earliest days, Bahá'í executives were members of the Chicago Rotary Club and later the Wilmette Rotary Club.

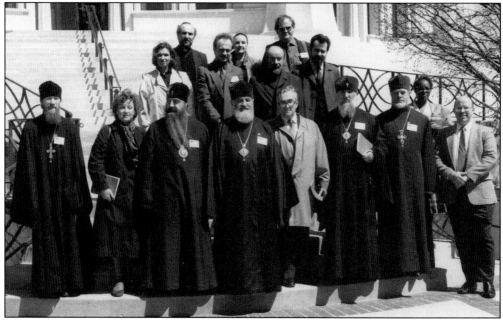

In 1986, the largest contingent of religious leaders was allowed outside the now-former Soviet Union to attend a conference of Russian and American clergy in Chicago. The 18 clergymen visiting the Temple represented the Russian Orthodox, Armenian Orthodox, Georgian Orthodox, Lutheran, and Baptist churches. Bahá'í literature in Russian at the Temple greatly impressed not only the clergymen, but also the representative of the National Council of Churches who had accompanied them.

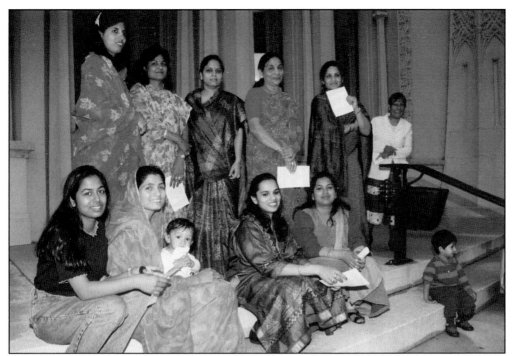

From India, Pakistan, Bangladesh, and other countries, South Asians living in Chicago are familiar visitors at the House of Worship. Whole families will enjoy an afternoon visit. The lovely saris worn by the ladies are always a pleasure to behold.

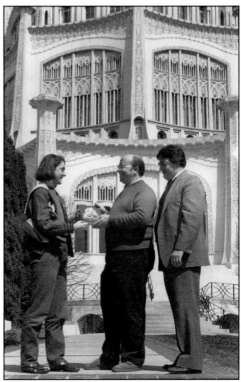

Bruce Whitmore and James Mock of the House of Worship's activities committee presented a copy of the *Dawning Place* to Sasha Pisarski, a high school senior from Park Ridge, Illinois. On March 30, 1984, she was the five millionth recorded visitor. The Temple's doors were first opened to visitors on May 1, 1931, and visitor counts have been tracked since June 1932. As of January 2010, there have been more than 10 million visitors.

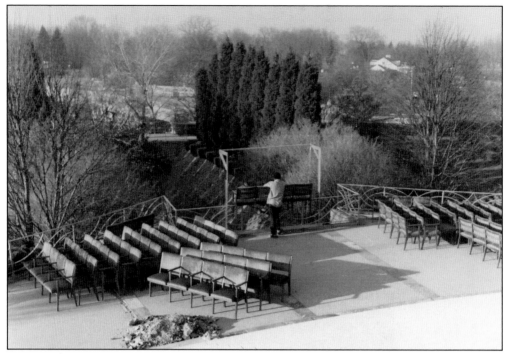

By 1974, the chairs in the auditorium had seen 20 years of use. Fred and Lola Baker, owners of Baker Interior Decoration Service in Gulfport, Mississippi, brought staff and equipment and set up shop in the foundation building. Each section of chairs was first brought out the doors and down the stairs to the terrace where a pulley lifted them farther down to the service entrance on the north side.

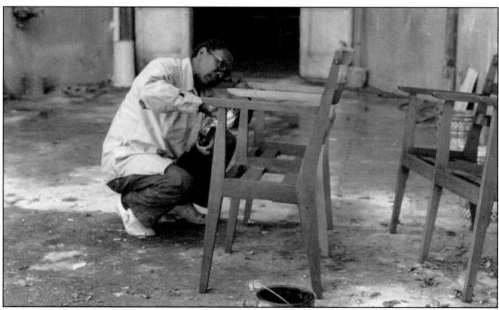

More than 1,190 chairs were checked for damage and wear. Old upholstery was stripped, the wood finish removed, repairs made, and then each chair refinished with lacquer. The maple chairs were reupholstered with 1,300 yards of antique taupe velvet.

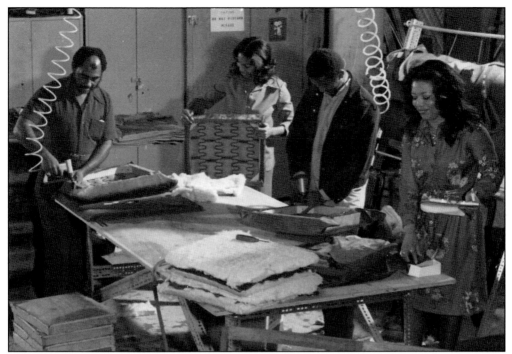

Fred and Lola brought their daughter, Amelia Baker, and James Davis from Mississippi to work with Robert Stoakley of Batavia, Illinois. The Bakers also redecorated rooms and repaired furniture at 536 Sheridan and 121 Linden Avenue, a home owned by the Bahá'ís. The Baker family returned in 1995 and again refinished and reupholstered every chair.

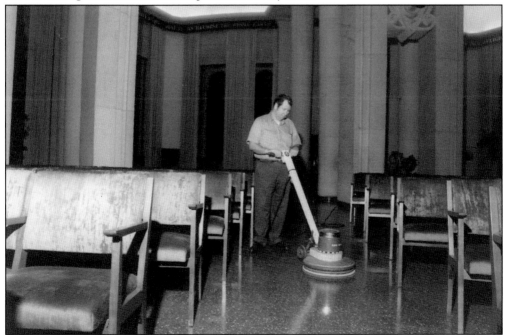

Underneath those handsome chairs in the auditorium is a rich red terrazzo floor that was kept cleaned and polished through many Chicago winters by longtime night janitor Ira Burget.

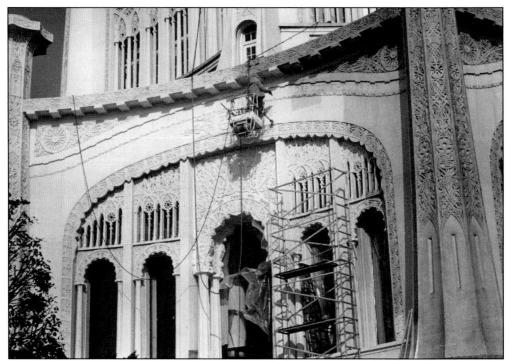

By the 1970s, the Temple was no longer very white. Dust, dirt, and air pollution had left a layer of grime over John Earley's beautiful concrete ornamental panels. Figuring out how to clean it was a difficult task. There was an attempt to use an acid wash, and then sandblasting, but these methods caused more harm than good.

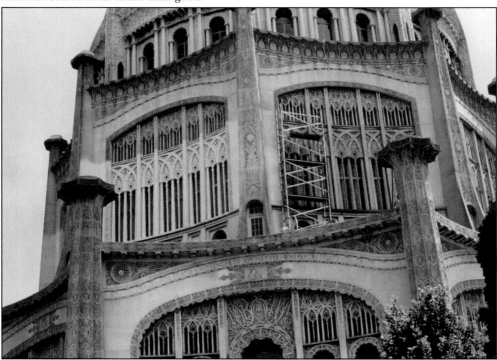

Nine

THE TEMPLE RESTORATION

By 1983, there was serious concern that age and wear had caused extensive damage to the Temple that would be difficult to repair. Clearly some pieces of ornamental concrete in the crown needed to be replaced, others needed to be repaired, and the entire building needed to be protected from future weathering. As consulting experts had always served the Temple well in the past, the National Spiritual Assembly invited 24 building professionals to meet, inspect the building from foundation to the top of the ribs, and decide together on a list of priorities. These were to repair the leaking skylight, replace the concrete base of the dome, and provide a thorough cleaning of the interior and exterior.

From 1984 to the present day, several restoration projects have been completed. This includes repairs to the original dome of Foundation Hall; additional support added to the steel structure; the ongoing replacement of the monumental stairs with installed heating systems to melt winter ice; and repairs that make the foundation building watertight, fixing leaks that have plagued the building for decades.

The terrace between the stairs and the gardens has been replaced in sections with a vault constructed underneath it to hold new mechanical systems for heating, cooling, plumbing, and electrical. The gardens are in the process of being restored to the original plan by Hilbert Dahl, and all nine fountains will be rebuilt. Six gardens have been completed with the final three under construction. In 2009, the small white buildings of 110 and 112 Linden were demolished, and ground is being prepared for a new visitor's center that will be appropriately accessible to people of all abilities.

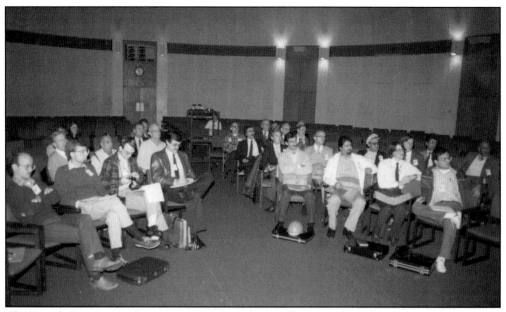

The Temple Restoration Seminar in 1983 brought together 23 architects, engineers, contractors, and project managers from throughout the United States and Canada to go over the Temple with a fine-toothed comb using state-of-the-art computer and digital technologies.

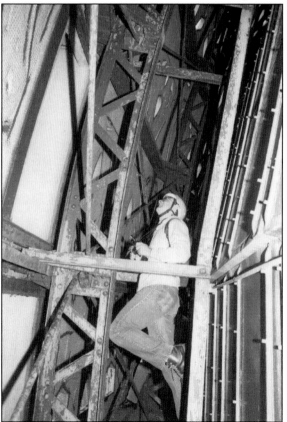

The steel structure between the ornamental concrete panels and the interior skylight was cleaned with water and sand and then treated with a protective coating to prevent further deterioration. Projected costs of replacing the 55-year-old skylights were more than a $1 million. Super Sky International suggested building a second skylight over the existing system, creating a waterproof and insulated system that saved money and protected against heat loss.

To clean the exterior of the building, a gentle spray of soap and water proved remarkably effective. Piping systems were set up to work automatically on the sides of the building, while workmen in extensive safety gear rappelled down the dome.

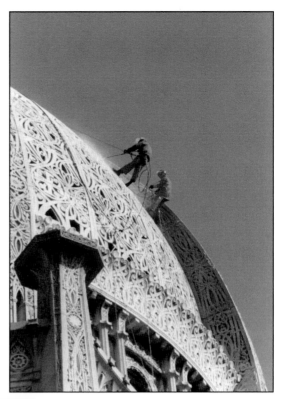

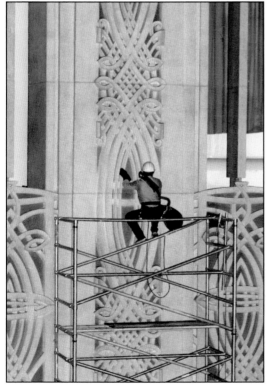

Forty years of dust was vacuumed from the interior ornamental concrete. Poultices removed 75 rust stains on the interior concrete caused by the leaking skylight.

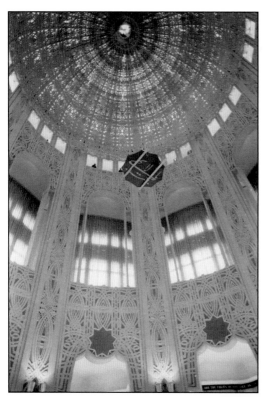

Restoration of the skylights was as good a time to clean up the simple piece of wood upon which is painted the prayer known to the Bahá'ís as the Greatest Name. For the first time since its installation in 1952, it was lowered 138 feet for painting and refurbishing. Notice the worker watching from the highest balcony to get an idea of the scale of the dome.

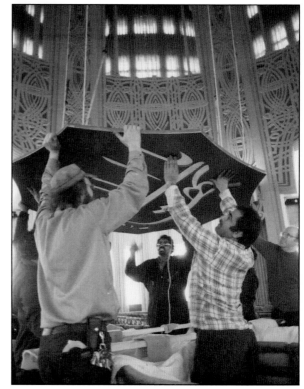

Maintenance crew members, along with former House of Worship administrator Bruce Whitmore, bring it down gently and are ready for some dusting and painting touch-ups.

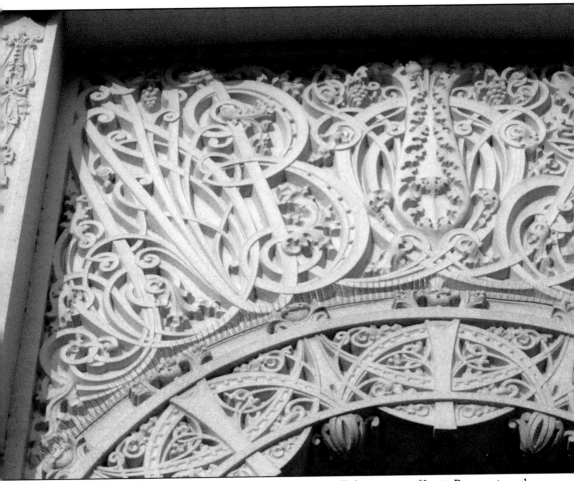

Within the sparkling clean ornamental panels can be seen all the artistry of Louis Bourgeois and the sculptors of the Earley Studio. In the panels directly above the nine doors, decorative letters, ABHA, of a word can be found. It is the Arabic word for glory; the word is also integral to the name of the prophet-founder of the Bahá'í Faith, Bahá'u'lláh, and the prayer called the Greatest Name. It is also an expression of the number nine. When the numbers representing the letters in Abha are added together according to the traditional Abjad numbering system they total nine (1+2+5+1). Numbers as representatives of spiritual concepts have a rich tradition in Islamic culture, and nine is the highest number symbolizing perfection, unity, and comprehensiveness. This is why a Bahá'í House of Worship features nine sides, doors, and gardens. (Courtesy of the Armbruster Company.)

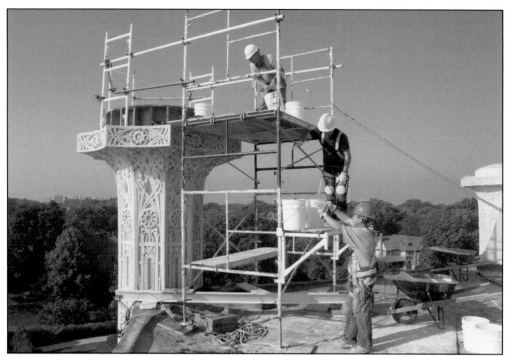

The original ornamental pylon caps and the first-story cornice had weaknesses in design and materials. New architectural concrete caps replaced the old crumbling pylon caps. Loaded wheelbarrows of concrete were sent up from below, making two stops on the way up via cranes and pulleys. (Courtesy of the Armbruster Company.)

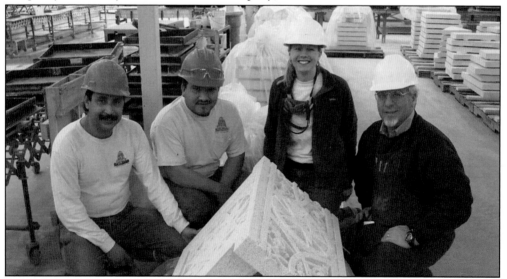

Just as the Earley Studio invented processes to use in constructing the Temple, so these processes were reinvented for making repairs. Shown here are Raul Millan, Roman Medina, Denise Armbruster, and Bob Armbruster of the Bahá'í–owned Temple Concrete Studio. This modern-day studio will design, craft, and cast the 9,000 pieces required for ongoing restoration projects. The studio is currently working on the restoration of other monuments designed by John Earley. (Courtesy of the Armbruster Company.)

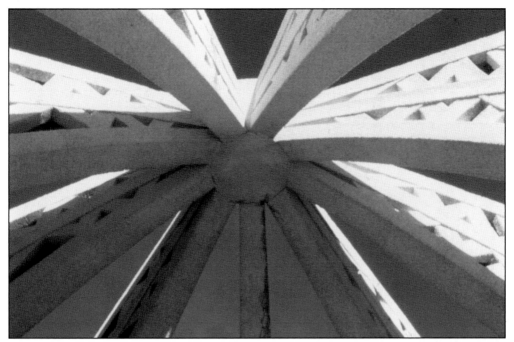

The ribs meet 17 feet over the Bahá'í Temple dome. While they show some wear, they are remarkably strong and secure. The restoration crews cleaned and then coated them with a sealant, which will protect the concrete for many years to come. (Courtesy of the Armbruster Company.)

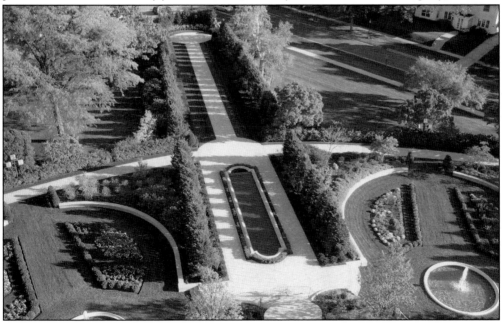

The restored gardens of the long approach now feature a reflecting pool, new fountains, the bench walls called for in Hilbert Dahl's plan, and a small entrance garden at the corner of Linden Avenue and Sheridan Road. The walks are now laid with paving stones instead of poured concrete, and the planting beds have been improved. The 50-year-old Chinese Juniper trees were replaced. (Courtesy of the Armbruster Company.)

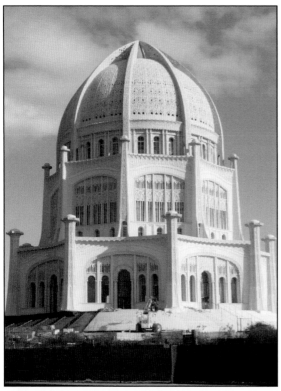

In anticipation of a new visitor's center, the small white buildings of 110 and 112 Linden Avenue were demolished in November 2009, giving visitors a 1940s-era view of foundation building. Stairs have been removed, so the structure underneath can be repaired and made waterproof. Automatic heating systems will be installed to eliminate the need for salt (and shoveling) during winter snows.

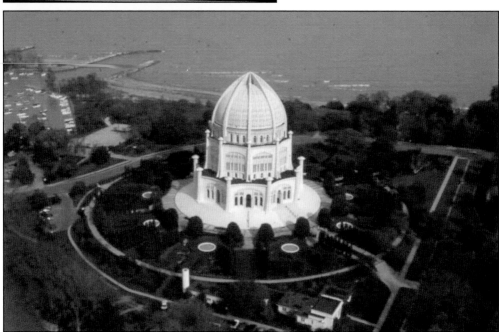

After a thorough cleaning in 1991, the Temple shines bright as it has not done since the 1940s. Future views will show a new visitor's center, beginning construction in 2012. From the day Nettie Tobin dragged a stone to this property in 1908, a Temple has been in progress. Perhaps it is never meant to be fully complete—like a prayer that does not end.

ABOUT THE BAHÁ'Í HOUSE OF WORSHIP

The Bahá'í House of Worship in Wilmette, Illinois, is open 365 days a year, with extended hours in the summer months. A devotional program is scheduled upstairs in the auditorium everyday at 12:30 p.m. that all are welcome to attend. A visitor's center downstairs features a bookstore, viewing room for media presentations, and a comfortable area for tours to meet. Information about the Bahá'í Faith is available in dozens of languages. To learn more about the Bahá'í Faith, the history of the Bahá'í House of Worship, to check visiting hours, or to arrange a tour, go to www.bahai.us/bahai-temple.

DISCOVER THOUSANDS OF LOCAL HISTORY BOOKS
FEATURING MILLIONS OF VINTAGE IMAGES

Arcadia Publishing, the leading local history publisher in the United States, is committed to making history accessible and meaningful through publishing books that celebrate and preserve the heritage of America's people and places.

Find more books like this at
www.arcadiapublishing.com

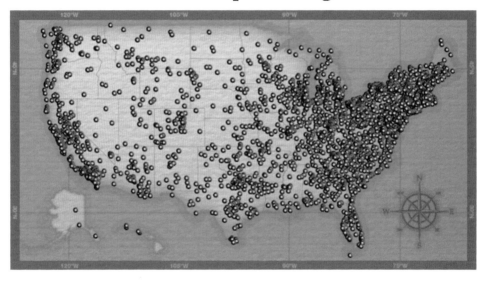

Search for your hometown history, your old stomping grounds, and even your favorite sports team.

Consistent with our mission to preserve history on a local level, this book was printed in South Carolina on American-made paper and manufactured entirely in the United States. Products carrying the accredited Forest Stewardship Council (FSC) label are printed on 100 percent FSC-certified paper.

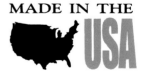
MADE IN THE USA